First Published 1993

ISBN 0-85516-088-8
ISSN 0268-1307

The Royal United Services Institute for Defence Studies (RUSI) is a professional body based in London dedicated to the study, analysis and debate of issues affecting defence and international security.

Founded in 1831 by the Duke of Wellington, the RUSI is one of the most senior institutes of its kind in the world which, throughout its history, has been at the forefront of contemporary political-military thinking through debates, public and private seminars, conferences, lectures and a wide range of publications. The independence of the Institute is guaranteed by a large, worldwide membership of those people and organisations who have a serious and professional interest in the thorough and objective analysis of defence and international security.

Critical and acclaimed analysis of issues of moment has underwritten the RUSI's Whitehall Papers for many years. The new series will, in its revised A5 monograph format, continue to provide expertise in the field. The series, which will comprise six publications a year, will address the major areas of current interest.

Whitehall Papers are available as part of a membership package, or singly at £6.50 plus p & p (£1.00 in the UK/ £2.00 overseas). Orders should be sent to the Publications Department, RUSI, Whitehall, London SW1A 2ET and cheques and postal orders made payable to the RUSI.

Printed in Great Britain by Sherrens Printers, Units 1 & 2, South Park, Granby Industrial Estate, Weymouth, Dorset.
The Royal United Services Institute for Defence Studies, Whitehall, London SW1A 2ET.
Registered Charity No. 210639

CONTENTS

Pax Russica: Russia's Monroe Doctrine   1

The Baltic States   27

The Core States   37

Russia and Transcaucasia   52

Conclusion   61

NOTE ON THE AUTHOR

Dr Mark Smith is a research fellow at the RUSI where he runs the Russian and Central European Programme. He completed a D Phil in Soviet-Latin American relations at St Antony's College, Oxford in 1988.

PAX RUSSICA: RUSSIA'S MONROE DOCTRINE

There are few who would dispute that the Soviet Union was, essentially, a Russian empire.[1] The leadership of the Soviet Union has been dominated by Russians since the inception of the Soviet state. The leadership of the Soviet armed forces was also largely Russian. In the period following the Second World War, the official Marxist Leninist doctrine was strongly tinged with the hue of Russian nationalism that reflected the outlook of the Russian leadership of the USSR. This leadership identified its motherland with the entire Soviet Union, and saw it as essential that it remain undivided.

Soviet strategic thinking (which is synonymous with Russian strategic thinking) saw Eastern Europe as a strategic glacis protecting the USSR against any potential military threat from the West. By extension, Soviet/Russian strategic thinking saw the non-Russian regions of the Soviet Union as a further glacis, providing further security for the Russian heartland, the core of the Soviet Union. The former Soviet Union can therefore be conceived of as a 'Russian defence zone'. The Russian heartland's links with the non-Russian territories was reinforced by the existence of sizeable Russian diaspora. By the late 1980s, some 25-30 million Russians lived in the non-Russian union republics.[2]

It is useful to examine the situation in the Soviet Union at the end of 1990, when the country began to break up, in order to be able to realise the anxiety that this disintegration evoked among the Soviet political elite, which was largely Russian in its ethnic composition. This will enable one to understand more clearly the perception of loss felt by many in the current Russian political elite as it seeks to come to terms with the emergence of newly independent states on the territory of the former USSR.

In 1990, the last full year of the Soviet Union's existence, the spectre of national disintegration loomed ever larger as a result of the 'parade of sovereignties', in which every union republic declared sovereignty and claimed that its authority took precedence over that of the all union centre in Moscow. In this way, the cohesion of the Russian defence zone was undermined. It was becoming more difficult for the Soviet armed forces (ie. the defenders of the Russian defence zone) to act as a coherent unit. Draft avoidance was increasing in the non-Russian republics, and some republican authorities were insistent on determining where their conscripts should be deployed.[3]

In view of this process of national disintegration, it was hardly surprising that the leaders of the Soviet security lobby became alarmed at the end of 1990, and emphasised the need to hold the country together. Gorbachev's move to increase the powers of the Soviet presidency in December 1990 aimed at increasing Moscow's control over the Soviet Union. In December 1990 the chairman of the KGB, Vladimir Kryuchkov, said the 'threat of the collapse of the Soviet Union has emerged', and blamed national chauvinism and the subversive actions of foreign special services for destroying the unity of the Soviet state.[4] He repeated this warning later in December, and warned that blood might have to be spilled to hold the Soviet state together.[5]

Colonel General G F Krivoshev, the deputy chief of the USSR Armed Forces General Staff, warned that 'attempts to undermine the armed forces as one of the most stable foundations of our state, have become...systematic and organised. We have reached the point where safeguarding the defence of the Soviet Union is not just the concern of the defence ministry but of everyone who cares about the future of our country.'[6] The Soviet defence minister Dmitry Yazov criticised in late November the moves of some republics to set up their own army units, and said that it was necessary to maintain the USSR armed forces as a single entity.[7] In his new year's message to troops at the end of 1990, Yazov again attacked national separatist forces, and asserted that the USSR Armed Forces represented a united combat family and that the officers and men of the Soviet armed forces regarded it as their sacred duty to strengthen their common home, the USSR.[8]

By the insistence that these individuals from the armed forces and internal security forces placed on retaining the unity of the Soviet state, it is clear that they saw the existence of the USSR as strategically vital. Krivoshev saw the maintenance of single armed forces as necessary to maintain parity with the US and NATO. 'If the armed forces are distributed among separate national compartments, this parity will inevitably be lost.'[9] Jerry Hough's warning in 1980 about the Soviet military's probable response to liberal reforms in the USSR seemed extremely appropriate. He commented that 'nationalist parties would most likely arise within the republics, and many of these might well choose independence. Therefore, democratisation would undoubtedly result in a great reduction in the national power of Russia, and would sharply bring to the fore the question of whether and how Russia would use military force 'to preserve the union'.[10]

The abortive coup that was staged against Gorbachev in August 1991 was launched largely to prevent the break up of the Soviet Union.[11] Following the coup's collapse, the Soviet Union broke up into its 15 constituent union republics, all of them becoming independent sovereign states. The Russian Federation, by virtue of its size, stands out as the largest, strongest and most significant of these successor states. The leadership of the Russian Federation was reluctant to see the union end. Although Yeltsin had fought resolutely in 1990 and early 1991 to strengthen the position of the Russian Federation *vis à vis* the union centre, and had weakened that centre by concluding bilateral treaties between the Russian Federation and other union-republics, neither he, nor the Russian leadership desired to see the union break up. Yeltsin supported the Novo Ogarevo process towards creating a new looser union in April 1991, and Russia supported the union treaty that was to be have been signed in August 1991.

After the coup collapsed in August, the Russian leadership continued to support the idea of a union treaty, and Yeltsin backed the new draft union treaty presented in November 1991.[12] At that time, the main obstacle to a renewed union was Ukraine, and Yeltsin, along with Gorbachev and the leaders of the other republics that desired to sign a union treaty, appealed in an open letter to the Ukrainian parliament in October 1991 not to abandon the union.[13] The Russian Federation leadership was therefore a strong advocate of a renewed Soviet Union. It did not desire to see the other union republics break away from Moscow. In this regard at least, there was a certain convergence of viewpoints between the reactionaries who launched the August coup, reform communists such as Gorbachev, and ex-communists in the Russian Federation's leadership. All desired the retention of most of the territory of the former Soviet Union. Again reflecting the strategic thinking of Russians, with the union as an important base of Russian great power status.

Since December 1991, the Russian Federation has had to deal with the strategic consequences of the break up of the union, and the loss of its strategic glacis. The Commonwealth of Independent States (CIS) which was set up in December 1991, aimed at overcoming this strategic loss by establishing a close framework for cooperation between independent states. The original document of the CIS signed in Minsk between Russia, Ukraine and Belarus in December envisaged close cooperation in the field of foreign and security policy. Article six of the Minsk agreement stated that:

• The member states of the community will preserve and maintain under united command a common military strategic space, including unified control over nuclear weapons...

Article seven of the agreement emphasised the need for close cooperation in the sphere of foreign policy. It stated that:

• The high contracting parties recognise that within the sphere of their activities, implemented on the equal basis through the common coordinating institutions of the commonwealth, will be the following:

• Cooperation in the sphere of foreign policy;

• Cooperation in forming and developing the united economic area, the common European and Eurasian markets, in the area of customs policy...

Article five of the agreement also noted that CIS members would 'respect one another's territorial integrity and the inviolability of existing borders within the commonwealth.'[14]

The reference to a 'common military strategic space' strongly implies that the now independent states of the former Soviet Union should form a common geo-political entity. In its political programme, for example, the Civic Union refers to the territory of the former USSR as a 'unified geo-political space'. The concepts of 'common military strategic space', 'unified geo-political space' occurred frequently in the writings and speeches of Soviet military leaders after the failure of the August coup, when they were confronted with the likelihood of the break up of the USSR. These concepts should be seen as the equivalent of the Russian defence zone, which the CIS was intended to preserve.

Some elements in the Russian leadership saw the CIS as a stepping stone to closer association. In mid-December 1991, Gennady Burbulis, who was then first deputy prime minister, said that 'confederation is a myth, it is a liberal illusion that can lead either to a federation or to war. And this is precisely the choice we are faced with'. He also foresaw that any coordinating bodies set up by the CIS would eventually turn into governing structures. This would effectively make the CIS into a state, rather than a loose association of states.[15] The CIS would become an ersatz union, replacing Gorbachev's proposed Union of Sovereign States as the successor to the old Soviet Union. In this way the Russian defence zone could be maintained.

In the military sphere, the general purpose forces of the USSR became the general purpose forces of the CIS. The Soviet defence minister, Marshal Evgenny Shaposhnikov, became the commander in chief of the CIS forces, while the Soviet command structure was transformed into the CIS command structure. While individual member states were granted the right to create their own armed forces, Russia and several other states initially intended to maintain former Soviet (now CIS) armed forces. In other words, a supranational armed force would remain, so ensuring the security of the defence space of the former Soviet Union.

However, the foundation of the CIS and the decision to retain the bulk of the Soviet armed forces as a supranational entity (which would inevitably be dominated by Russia) did not succeed in binding the CIS close to Russia. The disputes with Ukraine, which began in January 1992 following Kiev's decision to introduce a Ukrainian military oath, underlined the fragility of CIS. The notion of maintaining CIS armed forces became untenable, and Russia was forced to abandon this notion and so declared its intention to create its own armed forces in May 1992. While the CIS failed to grow into a tightly knit cohesive body, Moscow was unable to ensure that it could retain its strategic glacis.

This meant that Moscow, in the form of the Russian Federation, had suffered a serious strategic loss. In the space of a few months, with the end of the Soviet Union, it had lost 5.3 million square kilometres of territory, and almost 139 million citizens. The 25-30 million Russian citizens residing in the rest of the former Soviet Union were now under the rule of foreign leaders. The Russian military leadership had suffered considerably as a result of the break up of the Soviet armed forces. Approximately one half of combat aircraft, tanks and armoured vehicles, one fourth of warships and 44 per cent of the personnel of the former USSR's armed forces were located outside the borders of the Russian Federation.[16] Some of the most advanced Soviet military equipment was located in the western regions of the Soviet Union, and was therefore 'lost' when Belarus and Ukraine took control of the Soviet forces stationed on their territory. The Russian defence minister, General Pavel Grachev, claims that some 70 per cent of the most advanced technology and weapons of the USSR armed forces remained outside Russia when the Soviet Union broke up.[17] One of the most important military losses for the Russian military leadership has been the break up of the old Soviet air defence system.[18]

The demise of the Soviet Union thus leaves the Russian Federation with an acute sense of vulnerability, and a sense of reduced status in the world. Moscow's loss of the old communist empire in Eastern Europe was a substantial strategic and psychological blow to the ruling elite in Moscow, but Eastern Europe was regarded as foreign territory and so not comparable to the loss of territories that have been considered Russian for generations. The post-Soviet Russian foreign policy doctrine puts a significant dividing line between the states of the ex-Soviet Union and other foreign states, regarding the former as the 'near abroad' (*blizhnye zarubezhnye*), and the latter as the 'far abroad' (*dal'nye zarubezhnye*). This concept underlines the Russian notion that these states are 'special'.

Russia's loss of great power status is something that has been forcibly expressed by nationalist communist movements such as the National Salvation Front, which rejects the foreign policy changes wrought by both Gorbachev and Yeltsin, and desires a restoration of the USSR, with a return to the foreign policies of the pre-1985 era. It has also been expressed by individuals closer to the current Russian leadership, such as vice president Alexander Rutskoy, who made an interesting observation in December 1991. He argued that 'in 1984 the Soviet Union was a great power, and its army was a mighty force, a factor of peace and stability in the world. But what happened then was veritable disintegration of the state and of course disintegration of the army...'.[19] The belief that Russia should enjoy a great power status is a sentiment that is likely to be strongly felt by any Russian leadership, and if the Russian Federation is to aspire to this status in the future it will require an extremely close relationship with the 'near abroad'. Russian foreign minister Andrey Kozyrev feels that Russia cannot be a successful member of the international community without a close relationship with the ex-Soviet states. In July 1992 he stated: '...entry into the traditional international community will not be successful and sufficient for us if we are unable to create a real community of former Soviet republics.'[20]

Moscow's sense of strategic and psychological vulnerability has been expressed by many within Russia. One of the most influential political groups is the Civic Union, and its political programme 'Towards A United, Strong, and Democratic Russia', criticises the abolition of the USSR as a 'great miscalculation' by the current Russian leadership. It also reflects the loss felt as a result of the break up of the Soviet Union:

> Among the heaviest legacies of the disintegration of the communist empire is the fact that the territory of historical Russia was reduced to the boundaries of the 17th century. A large part of Russia's contemporary history, all that which comprises its historical memory and pride and formulates the national self awareness of the residents of Russia, turned out

7

to be beyond the limits of Russia's borders. Many of the acquisitions of historical Russia, especially in the west and the south, turned out to be under the control of national heirs to the communist empire, who hastened to announce the results of the party administrative tyranny regarding their state boundaries. From this standpoint, Russia turned out to be almost the only one of the former union republics which suffered serious territorial, economic and psychological losses.[21]

The Civic Union also argues that Russian security is directly dependent on the situation in the contiguous regions of the former USSR.[22] This sense of loss means that the Russian Federation is extremely unlikely to be a sated state. Rutskoy has argued that the historic borders of Russia cannot be automatically identified with the current borders of the Russian Federation.[23] He has also called for the restoration of a single democratic statehood on the territory of a more extensive (ie. more extensive than the Russian Federation) area.[24] The Civic Union's programme itself advocates that controversial territorial questions between Commonwealth states must be resolved.[25] Even current foreign minister Andrey Kozyrev, who opposes a heavy handed policy towards Russia's CIS neighbours, has said that it may be necessary to redraw Russia's borders.[26]

A major task for Russian foreign policy makers since the dissolution of the Soviet Union has been to define Russia's place in the international system as a whole, and also its place and role in the regional sub-system known as the former Soviet Union. Probably one of the most important attempts to conceptualise the Russian Federation's foreign policy interests was made by Sergey Rogov, the deputy director of the USA and Canada Institute of the Russian Academy of Sciences. He sees the Russian Federation's security interests as a set of three concentric circles.

The first circle comprises Russia's relations with the former Soviet republics. He warns of the danger of being pulled into territorial and national conflicts with these states, and argues that it is vitally important for Russia to develop 'friendly, preferably allied relations' with these states.

The second circle comprises regions such as Eastern Europe, the Near East and the Far East, areas that were traditionally within the sphere of interest of the USSR. Rogov argues that although Russia is separated from these regions by a belt of ex-Soviet states, Moscow cannot distance itself from these regions, otherwise the Russian Federation would be geo-politically isolated.

The third circle comprises the West, primarily the US and Western Europe. Rogov argues that Russia should establish close cooperative relations with these states, and that the CIS members could be natural partners of Russia in its pursuit of close ties with Western states. Rogov comments that 'aside from the coalition approach, Russia's military political relations with certain former republics of the USSR will have to be built on the basis of bilateral agreements also.'[27]

All those concerned with Russian foreign policy would agree that Rogov's first circle comprises Russia's foreign policy priority. The Civic Union's programme considers that:

> ...the territory of the former USSR is a sphere of specific vitally important Russian interests. This is based on a number of objective factors: the retained economic interdependence of states; the close scientific and cultural ties; a direct dependence of the security of Russia on the situation in the contiguous regions of the former USSR; the moral and political responsibility of Russia for the fate of the Russian speaking minorities; the exclusive role of Russia in curtailing the distribution and dissolution of the military arsenals of the former USSR (including nuclear weapons and their delivery systems); the natural status of Russia as the axis of military political stability in continental Eurasia.'

The Civic Union's conception is likely to be widely shared throughout the Russian foreign policy establishment. Like Rogov, the Civic Union advocates that Russia should cooperate with its ex-Soviet neighbours in ensuring security in bilateral and multilateral forms.

The emphasis that Russia and the former Soviet states are natural allies is repeated in the draft military doctrine presented by the Russian General Staff in May 1992. The doctrine argued that 'Russia proceeds from the assumption that its security is inseparable from that of the other Commonwealth states. The defence of Russia and of the Commonwealth as a whole can be ensured with greatest effectiveness by joint efforts of the CIS countries with centralised operational leadership of their collective defense.' The doctrine also states that 'Russia's main goal in a war imposed on it will be to defend its sovereignty and that of the Commonwealth states allied with it.' The doctrine assumes that there is an automatic identity of security interests between itself and the rest of the CIS.

The doctrine would also give Russia an effective veto over the security policy of other ex-Soviet states. Some of its premises may be seen as an implied threat to these states, in that it views 'the introduction of foreign troops on the territory of contiguous states as well as a build up of army and naval groupings as a direct military threat'. Taken to a logical conclusion, this would prevent any neighbouring state from forming an alliance with a third state without Russia's consent. A feature of the doctrine that has been controversial in the near abroad has been its emphasis on protecting the rights of Russians throughout the former USSR. It warned that 'a violation of the rights of Russian citizens and of persons who identify themselves with Russia culturally and ethnically in former USSR republics can be a serious source of conflicts.'

This doctrine has been criticised for failing to outline Russia's security needs with sufficient clarity. Colonel General Igor Rodionov, the director of the Academy of the General Staff, rejected any idea that the ex-Soviet states could form part of a buffer zone between Russia and the outside world. He argued instead that these states should be Russia's primary allies, and they should utilise the remaining elements of the old USSR defence system as a basis for military integration. Rodionov also stated that he would prefer the former Warsaw Pact states of Eastern Europe either to have a friendly relationship with Russia or 'in an extreme case' to adhere to a neutral status in international relations. By implication, any orientation by these states towards the West would be seen as a threat to Russian security interests.

The aversion to the ex-Soviet states developing close security or political ties with non-Soviet states is extremely widely held. The Civic Union attacks the idea of any distant foreign country creating spheres of influence or coalitions of powers on the territory of the former USSR as extremely dangerous, possibly leading to the 'disunification of the unified space and to new conflicts and instability.' This aversion is widespread throughout the Russian foreign policy establishment, and it appears that Moscow is of the opinion that the states of the former Soviet Union should be fundamentally oriented towards Moscow. There is a corresponding concern that foreign states are engaged in the process of building spheres of influence throughout the former USSR. These spheres are illegitimate in Moscow's eyes. The current chief of the Russian General Staff, Colonel General Mikhail Kolesnikov, has accused the West of seeking to divide the CIS. Kolesnikov argued that the US, NATO and Japan did not wish to see Russia emerge as a new centre of power on the territory of the former Soviet Union. He feared that armed conflicts in the territory of the former Soviet Union could lead to western intervention on the pretext of ensuring the security of the old USSR nuclear arsenal.[28]

In December 1992, Shaposhnikov attacked some CIS states for trying to create defence systems by their own efforts and for striving to integrate themselves into the NATO system. Shaposhnikov accused NATO of trying to split the Commonwealth. He claimed that 'if NATO officials have ever spoken of closer cooperation with certain CIS states, they did so wittingly or unwittingly in order to intensify disintegration processes within the Commonwealth.' He then expressed fears that Iran, Turkey and Pakistan were increasing their influence in various parts of the former union.[29]

Rogov fears that certain former republics could come under the influence of global and regional power centres such as Germany, China, Turkey or Iran. The CU's programme expresses concern that Central Asia is developing ties with 'distant foreign' countries. Leading political figures who would be considered as centrists within

Russia also take a similar view. The chairman of the Russian Supreme Soviet Defence and Security Committee, Sergey Stepashin, has accused the Baltic states of rigidly following a pro-American orientation, and emphasised the need for Russia to aid the Central Asian states in building their armed forces for fear that Turkey, Iran or Iraq will do so otherwise.[30]

Stepashin's fears of external powers acquiring influence in the former Soviet Union has been more graphically expressed by his counterpart on the Supreme Soviet Foreign Affairs Committee, Evgenny Ambartsumov. He warns that certain Turkish circles aim at building a 'Pan-Turkish empire from the Adriatic to the Urals and beyond to the Great Wall of China. Moreover they are counting on the support of the Muslims of the Volga region, the South Urals, and West Siberia.'[31] Elsewhere he has accused the US and Britain of 'imprudently stimulating' the growth of the Islamic factor in the regions south of the Russian Federation.[32] This corresponds with the Civic Union's fear that Russia's traditional alliances have been destroyed and that the 'ghosts of seemingly long buried empires began to be resurrected—the Ottoman, the Austro-Hungarian, and even the Germanic'.[33]

Moscow's fear of other states creating spheres of influence appears to be both quite genuine and accurate. The ending of Moscow's control over the ex-Soviet periphery has inevitably allowed 'distant foreign' states to expand their political and economic relationship with the ex-Soviet states. Russian perceptions of international relations in the former Soviet Union put a difference between the notion of spheres of influence, and spheres of interest. The former is ascribed to distant foreign states, and implies the establishment of an unequal satellite-type relationship between a powerful distant foreign state and less powerful clients in the former CIS. The sphere of interest concept applies to the Russian Federation's interests within the former Soviet Union, namely the desire to maintain close economic, political and strategic ties with the former Soviet states.

Russian observers argue that this can and must be done by non-imperial methods. The Civic Union advocates strengthening cooperation on a confederative basis through the CIS. It repudiates any form of imperial policy by Moscow towards its neighbours and rejects any form of *gendarme* role for Russia in the former USSR. Ambartsumov also rejects the concept of Russia as a *gendarme*. However, given the pressures for border revision in Russia, Moscow's concern about the political and military influence of foreign states in the former Soviet Union, and its concern to protect the rights of Russian citizens in the territory of former Soviet states, it is difficult to see how Russia can avoid pursuing a neo-imperial policy towards the former Soviet states. Russian policy is likely to be based on 'hegemonic presumption' that will aim at creating a Russian sphere of influence in the former Soviet Union.[34] Ambartsumov has called for the establishment of a Russian Monroe Doctrine,[35] and the Civic Union's programme calls for an American recognition of a Russian sphere of influence:

> Russia is ready to assume its part of the burden [of preventing conflicts], primarily in the geo-political space of the former USSR and the adjoining regions. We recognise the specific role of the USA in this sort of multilateral action in the regions of its vitally important interests, and expect the USA to take a similar approach toward the role of Russia on the basis of reciprocity.[36]

What sort of relationship is likely to emerge between Russia and its neighbours? This paper has referred to the notion of spheres of influence, but this concept needs to be considered carefully if Russia's policy towards the near abroad is to be clearly conceptualised. John Vloyantes has defined a sphere of influence as follows:

> A sphere of influence is an area into which is projected the power and influence of a country primarily for political, military strategic, or economic purposes...States within the area are usually nominally independent, but the degree of influence may be so great as to leave little independence; or it may be so indirect and restrained as to permit considerable independence. A sphere may be more or less exclusive, depending on the degree of independence states within it can enjoy.

A sphere of influence can also result from a special position of leadership, initiative, and direction by a great power in association with independent countries, arising out of mutually acceptable relationships which have been established.

A sphere of influence can also result from the activities of private economic entities (with more or less support from the home governments) when they become a significant factor in the life of a country.[37]

The ability of Russia to exercise influence over its neighbours will depend on the sort of state that emerges in Russia itself. The political future of the Russian Federation is highly uncertain. There appear to be three possible alternatives.

1. The Russian Federation falls apart into several small states. Yeltsin has warned that 50 or 60 principalities could emerge on the territory of the Russian Federation.[38] This is likely to be accompanied by several small wars between rival principalities. The Russian armed forces would also splinter. The centrifugal tendencies that currently exist in Russia indicate that this is a distinct possibility.

2. An authoritarian nationalist dictatorship emerges that is able to establish tight central control over the Russian Federation. This regime would probably be led by the 'red brown' forces that currently oppose Yeltsin's administration.[39]

3. The Russian Federation remains as it is at present, with the central government in Moscow exercising some control over its regions.

Only the second and third possibilities would appear to make it possible for Russia to pursue a relatively coherent foreign policy towards both the 'near foreign' and 'distant foreign' countries. It would appear impossible for any Russian leadership to be able to establish a replica of the relationship with the 'near abroad' that the USSR had with the Warsaw Pact states during the Cold War. Russia might strive to achieve the sort of relationship that existed between the Soviet Union and Finland during the Cold War, when there was a certain degree of deference by Helsinki towards Moscow over security policy. In other spheres Finnish foreign policy was independent of Moscow, and Finland was able to achieve a greater degree of foreign policy autonomy in relations with Moscow in the *detente* era of the 1960s and 1970s. Its internal politics were also mostly free from Soviet interference.[40]

However, Moscow may be able to exercise greater influence over some ex-Soviet states than the old Soviet Union ever exercised over Finland. It is not impossible, for example, that a hardline Russian leadership may intervene militarily in some states to pursue and protect its interests. In this respect, Russian policy may resemble US policy towards Central America in the early years of the twentieth century when the US intervened on several occasions in politically and economically unstable Caribbean states.[41]

The likely instruments of Russian policy comprise political, economic and military integration on both a multilateral and bilateral level. Any integration in the former Soviet Union which includes Russia is bound to be dominated by Moscow, due to Russia's sheer size in relation to the other ex-Soviet states. Ideally Russia would seek to establish a supranational EC-type relationship with the other CIS members, or at the very least close horizontal inter-state cooperation. Sergey Karaganov, the deputy director of the Institute of Europe of the Academy of Sciences, and since February 1993 a member of the Russian Presidential Council, envisages Russia's ties with its ex-Soviet states as an interlinking of political and economic penetration.

The key aspect of Russian strategy towards the countries of the former USSR should comprise the encouragement of the investment of private and public Russian capital. This should create a firm basis for future economic ties, and create additional channels of constructive political influence.[42]

As will be seen, there is strong evidence to suggest that this thinking is being reflected in official circles in Moscow. Multilateral relations have so far been conducted through the CIS, which has achieved various structures to facilitate economic, political and military cooperation. The most important documents signed to date have been the CIS Charter at the Minsk Heads of State summit in January 1993, and the collective security agreement concluded in Tashkent in May 1992. The charter outlines the various cooperative structures which have been established by the CIS members since December 1991.[43] It also prescribes the rules for interaction between the member states of the CIS.

The Tashkent treaty outlines the structures and mechanisms for collective self-defence of CIS members.[44] Like NATO, an attack on one member state of the treaty organisation is regarded as an attack on all, and all other states will render assistance (including military assistance) to that state. Alongside these multilateral structures exist the bilateral friendship and cooperation treaties that Russia has either concluded or is negotiating with the 14 other ex-Soviet republics. Only three of the signatories (including Russia) have so far ratified the treaty.[45]

The CIS High Command has a staff of about 300 and began work on 1 September 1992. Its role and structures were worked out at the CIS heads of state summit in Moscow on 6 July. It has four main functions: unified control and management of strategic missile forces; the coordination of military doctrines and military reform programmes of CIS members; crisis and conflict management within the CIS. It is envisaged that the CIS will have forces under its operational command that can react to particular conflicts, and intelligence analysis of the politico-military situation to make policy recommendations and proposals 'at the highest level'.[46]

The High Command comprises personnel from all CIS armed forces. The CIS Commander in Chief is subordinated to the Council of Heads of State and the Council of Defence Ministers. The commanders of various arms of the Russian armed forces will become deputies of the CIS Commander-in-Chief as over 80 per cent of the air force, navy and air defence infrastructure belong to Russia. However, the CIS military structures are likely to be subordinate to Russia, and will probably serve as an instrument enabling Russia to order the military affairs of the Tashkent agreement. The most important aspect to date of the CIS military structures has been the coordination of peacekeeping missions in the CIS.[47]

These agreements and arrangements give a very imperfect picture of Russia's relations with its neighbours. They certainly denote a desire by all the signatories to establish a close relationship, but they say little more than that: they convey no impression of the hegemonic relationship that Russian policymakers envisage. Similarly the 1955 treaty establishing the Warsaw Pact conveyed no impression of the reality of the Soviet East European relationship. A clearer indication comes from the actions and statements of Russian policymakers. As discussed above, in view of Russia's sheer size, it would be extremely difficult, if not impossible, for Russia not to establish a hegemonic type relationship with most of the ex-Soviet states.[48]

The ongoing debate within Russia about the approach that should be adopted towards the ex-Soviet republics has been one of the most important foreign policy debates within the Russian Federation since the dissolution of the USSR. It may be seen as a dialogue between advocates of a 'loose hegemony' and 'tight hegemony'.

The foremost advocate of the loose hegemony approach has been Russia's foreign minister Andrey Kozyrev. He sees Russian policy towards the 'near abroad' as aiming at creating a 'belt of good-neighbourliness', which includes forging equal but nonetheless special relationships with the former Soviet republics and strengthening the CIS as an international organisation.[49] Kozyrev rejects using force or the language of force to protect the interests of Russian communities in other non-Soviet states.[50] He has on occasion opposed renegotiating borders between former Soviet states, although his stance has not been consistent.[51] Along with Kozyrev, another strong advocate of a loose hegemony was the former first deputy foreign minister, Fedor Shelov-Kovedaev, who stepped down in October 1992.[52]

The advocates of 'tight hegemony' have become more influential in Moscow since early 1992. They are more numerous than the former school, and likely to become still more influential. The most prominent advocate is vice president Alexander Rutskoy, who has stated that 'once the Russian flag has been raised it should never be lowered'.[53] Also of this school are the chairman of the Supreme Soviet, Ruslan Khasbulatov, the chairman of the Foreign Affairs

Committee of the Supreme Soviet, Evgenny Ambartsumov, and Sergey Stankevich, one of Yeltsin's key political advisers, plus the Russian military leadership.[54] This school favours a much more assertive approach towards protecting the interests of the Russian diaspora throughout the 'near abroad'.

This diaspora is not confined to the 25-30 million Russians living outside the Russian Federation, but includes all individuals living outside the republic of their titular nationality.[55] The 'tight hegematists' also favour revising Russia's borders, and are particularly reluctant to accept Ukrainian independence.[56] The use of economic sanctions and, if necessary, military force against ex-Soviet states is favoured by some advocates of this school.[57]

The 'tight hegemony' school is gaining ground over its 'loose hegemony' counterpart. Kozyrev has shifted away from his original position and moved closer to the position of his critics. He has argued that border changes may be necessary, provided they are altered in accordance with CSCE principles. In June 1992 Kozyrev spoke of the possibility of Crimea returning to Russian rule, and the Dnestr region in Moldavia becoming part of Russia.[58] In March 1993 he accused the three Baltic states of violating the rights of their Russian communities, and warned that a 'new Yugoslavia' might erupt which would require the dispatch of peacekeeping troops.[59] In taking this stance, Kozyrev is trying to deflect the pressure exerted on him by nationalist forces within the Supreme Soviet who desire his removal. It is therefore a tactical manoeuvre on his part rather than a heartfelt conversion to the views of his opponents. Kozyrev's shift does nevertheless indicate the strength of the neo-imperial lobby, and it will be increasingly difficult to oppose this trend in Russia.

The increased emphasis on a tighter CIS is partially connected with the broader foreign policy debate in Russia, which Sergey Stankevich has depicted as a debate between Atlanticists and Eurasianists. The Atlanticists desire that Russia should become an integral member of the western community and join western international organisations such as NATO, the G7 and EC. The Eurasian school, which Stankevich supports, favours an eastwards shift in Russian policy towards its neighbours on the Eurasian land mass. This includes the other former Soviet states, and countries such as India, China and the Southeast Asian states. The Eurasian school rejects the Atlanticist approach as it is seen as condemning Russia to the role of junior partner of the West. Stankevich combines his advocacy of Eurasianism with a call for a more assertive defence of Russians in the 'near abroad'. He argues that 'the response to any discriminatory decision or action in respect to the Russian population and, more broadly, the Russian heritage, should be rule No.1 of both our embassies in our near neighbours and of our Foreign Ministry.' He says that Russia has so far shown 'insufficient diplomatic assertiveness' over this issue and that the country should 'adopt a tougher tone than has been the case hitherto.'[60]

This notion of Eurasianism has become a more prominent feature of Russian foreign policy. When Yeltsin visited India in January 1993, he saw the development of ties with India, China, South Korea and Japan as balancing Russia's *Westpolitik*. Yeltsin said that the West had not responded negatively to this development, but conceded that this was possible in the future.[61] On the eve of Yeltsin's visit to China in December 1992, deputy foreign minister Georgy Kunadze described Russia's task as expanding 'our diplomacy in the Asian Pacific region, thereby placing Russian foreign policy on two firm foundations...one being our ties with the West, the other being our ties with the East.'[62] During his visit to China, Yeltsin described Russia as 'a great Eurasian power' that wants balanced relations with Europe and Asia alike.[63]

Yeltsin's greater interest in Asia has been accompanied by criticisms of the Russian foreign ministry for its supineness in protecting Russian interests. He felt that Russia had come to be perceived as a power that only ever says 'Yes', and then continued by criticising the West for failing to support adequately Russia's reforms.[64] The greater emphasis on Eurasia is not intrinsically anti-Western, but it does suggest a somewhat diminished interest in the West, and in relation to the ex-Soviet Union, a stronger desire to consolidate this region as a Moscow-oriented bloc.

This move has grown stronger throughout 1993. The CIS Charter can be regarded as a first step towards closer integration. In March,

Yeltsin outlined in greater detail his vision of closer cooperation between the CIS states. He said that:

> Russia confirms anew its determined support for the commonwealth. Whilst laying no claim to the 'leading' role in it, we realise our responsibility for ensuring that we cooperate closely and on an equal basis with all the independent states in the interests of economic and social recovery, in order to secure the stability and security in our common geo-political space, which is so needed by each one of us. We are convinced that only by joint efforts can the independent states emerge from their difficulties and tribulations.[65]

It is significant that Yeltsin incorporates the term 'common geo-political space' in his statement, so echoing a concept which appeared in the Civic Union's political programme.

Yeltsin proposed improved cooperation in the spheres of foreign and security policy, and called for the creation of collective peacekeeping forces. His views on economic cooperation are perhaps the most significant. He said:

> The past year has confirmed the pressing need to undertake more energetically the arrangement of multilateral economic cooperation. It is no secret that the current state of affairs in virtually all our countries and the real economic potential of individual states do not make it possible for us solely to rely on our own efforts to extricate ourselves from the crisis. The combining of efforts—both within the commonwealth and on a bilateral basis—will increase greatly the effect of the reforms and changes being carried out.

He then spoke on the various forms of cooperation that he would like to see the CIS states develop:

> In the new conditions we shall also need new forms of cooperation, for example, the creation of trans-national associations in the various branches of industry, agriculture,

electric power, transport and services. The establishment of horizontal links, joint activity in production and investment and the formation of joint customs systems and free trade zones will help us to stabilise the economic situation, shape a single economic space and, in the long term, move towards a common market.[66]

These cooperation proposals reflect the Russian desire to tie economically the 'near abroad' to the Russian Federation. This would thus increase the dependence of these states on Russia, and so make it more difficult for them to pursue foreign policies that Moscow might consider anti-Russian. In March 1993, Yury Shafranik, the Russian minister for fuel and power engineering, urged the former Soviet republics to invest hundreds of billions of roubles in the Russian oil industry, otherwise by 1995 Russia would be able to ensure only its domestic requirements for fuel;[67] Indeed all former Soviet states except Estonia, Latvia and Turkmenistan, signed an agreement to create an intergovernmental council on oil and gas. This move parallels the USSR's drive to encourage the East European states to invest in the extraction of Soviet raw materials in the 1980s.[68]

This attempt at greater economic integration in order to bind the 'near abroad' more closely to the Russian economy is also connected with the notion of economic sanctions. This has been spoken of in Russia in relation to ex-Soviet states that mistreat their Russian communities. In speaking of ties with other ex-Soviet states, Rutskoy has said that the 'Soviet Union was a large dairy cow that was fed in Russia and milked in other republics'. He later commented that 'rigorous economic sanctions must be taken into consideration' against states that violated the rights of Russians.[69] In July 1992 he expressed this idea in graphic fashion in *Komsomolskaya Pravda*:

> Wherever the genocide of the Russian speaking population is patently obvious and people are attempting to wipe their feet on Russia, my method is as follows: A strip of land is plowed up, a border is established, we congratulate [the countries] on their independence and sovereignty, and everything, gas, timber, coal and the rest, becomes available for hard currency only. Two months later they themselves

come crawling and say that they no longer want sovereignty and will no longer disparage the Russians.[70]

In June 1992 Rutskoy criticised other former union republics for failing to meet their economic obligations to Russia, even though Russia supplies 90 per cent of their energy and accounts for 70 per cent of their trade.[71]

The use of economic leverage now appears to have become official policy. Such thinking was expressed by Russian prime minister Viktor Chernomyrdin in March 1993:

> ...we shall be building up our economic relations and helping our partners out when they need it, but only if the legal rights of the Russian speaking population and the Russian citizens are being strictly observed by them. And this includes the rights of Russian servicemen.[72]

As the trade dependence of most ex-Soviet states on the Russian Federation is quite high, Moscow possesses an economic lever that could be quite effective. Figures released in August 1992 state that Russia accounts for 79 per cent of Ukraine's exports, 69 per cent of Belarus' exports and 68 per cent of Kazakhstan's. Russia itself imports 6.4 per cent of its total consumption from other CIS countries, and exports 6.6 per cent of its output to CIS countries.[73] Russia has also suffered economically from selling oil and gas to other republics at prices below world levels. If it increased these prices to world levels, it would subsequently acquire a significant lever for use against the 'near abroad'. Moscow's temptation to use this weapon is likely to grow, and Russia is likely to view anxiously attempts by the states of the 'near abroad' to orient their economies away from Moscow, and the perception of 'economic penetration' by states from the 'far abroad' is likely to emerge in Russian strategic thinking. If the Russian Federation is able to survive as a coherent entity, then its economic ties with its neighbours will play an important role in building a sphere of influence.

The following section will examine Russia's policies towards its fourteen neighbours in the 'near abroad'. It will consider Russia's perceptions of these states, and the dynamics of Moscow's relationships with them.

1 Alexander Solzhenitsyn rejects this idea, arguing that the USSR was a Communist empire, rather than Russian. See his 'Misconceptions about Russia are a threat to America', *Foreign Affairs*, Vol. 58, No. 4, Spring 1980, pp.797-834, especially p.812. See also John Dunlop 'Russia: confronting a loss of empire' in Ian Bremmer and Ray Taras eds. *Nations and Politics in the Soviet Successor States* (CUP, Cambridge, 1993), pp.45-74.
2 The last Soviet census was carried out in 1989. For information on the national composition of the USSR's population see *Natsional'ny sostav naseleniya SSSR, Finansy i statistika*, Moskva, *1991*. A useful summary is provided in *The Firstbook of Demographics for the republics of the former Soviet Union 1951*-1990 (Shady Side Maryland, New World Demographics, 1992).
3 In November 1990 Colonel General G F Krivoshev, the then deputy chief of the USSR Armed Forces General Staff, attacked republican authorities for adopting unconstitutional measures that hindered recruitment and the draft. See *Krasnaya Zvezda*, 23 November 1990. In *Pravitelstvenny Vestnik* no.48, November 1990, Prizyvnikii, piketchiki, otkazniki... Krivoshev gives details of the extent of draft avoidance in the non-Russian republics.
4 *FBIS SOV 90* 239, 12 December 1990, p.32-33.
5 *FBIS SOV 90* 247, 24 December 1990, p.30.
6 *Krasnaya Zvezda*, 23 November 1990.
7 *FBIS SOV 90* 229, 28 November 1990, p.68.
8 *Krasnaya Zvezda*, 31 December 1990.
9 *FBIS SOV 90* 232, 3 December 1990, p.73.
10 Jerry F Hough *Soviet Leadership in Transition* (Brookings, Washington D.C, 1980), p.35.
11 In *Sovetskaya Rossiya*, 23 July 1991, several prominent figures, including the commander of the USSR Ground Forces, Valentin Varennikov, and first deputy interior minister Boris Gromov issued an appeal calling for the armed forces to act to save the collapse of the nation.
12 *Izvestiya*, 26 November 1991.
13 *Krasnaya Zvezda*, 23 October 1991.
14 All these principles were incorporated into the CIS Charter signed in Minsk in January 1993. See *Rossiskaya Gazeta*, 12 February 1993.
15 Burbulis eventually saw the former Soviet republics returning Moscow's fold. In March 1992 he said 'there is a logic that will bring the

former Soviet republics back again to our way. Europe will not take them as they are': cited by John Lough 'The Place of the 'Near Abroad' in Russian Foreign Policy in *RFE/RL Research Report*, Vol.2, No.11, 12 March 1993, p.25, fn.29.

16 See the article by Sergey Rogov in *Moskovskie Novosti*, No.2, 5-12 January 1992, p.5 in *FBIS SOV* 92 015, 23 January 1992, pp.18-19.

17 *Rossiskie Vesti*, 4 January 1993.

18 Shaposhnikov informed the Congress of Peoples' Deputies in December 1992 that 'the destruction of a single anti-aircraft defence system results in whole regions, includng the Caucasus and Tajikistan, finding themselves only partially protected.' BBC, *SWB* SU/1563 C2/4 14 December 1992.

19 *Krasnaya Zvezda*, 27 December 1991.

20 *Izvestiya*, 24 July 1992.

21 'Towards A United, Strong, and Democratic Russia', 1992.

22 *Ibid.*

23 *Pravda*, 30 January 1992.

24 *Nezavisimaya Gazeta*, 13 February 1992.

25 *Op. cit.*, 'Towards a...'

26 *Le Monde*, 7-8 June 1992.

27 Sergey Rogov 'Rossiya i SShA v mnogopolyarnom mire', *SSHA: Ekonomika, Politika, Ideologiya*, October 1992, pp.8-9.

28 *The Independent*, 1 August 1992.

29 BBC, *SWB* SU/1563 C2/4, 14 December 1992.

30 *Izvestiya*, 23 December 1992.

31 See the interview with Ambartsumov in *Narodny Deputat*, No.16, 1992, p.18.

32 See Ambartsumov's article 'Russia As a Great Power: From Megalomania to Common Sense' in *Literaturnaya Gazeta* No.44, 28 October 1992. Ambartsumov also accuses Germany of expanding its influence throughout the former Soviet Union.

33 *Ibid.*

34 Abraham F. Lowenthal used this term to describe US Latin American relations. See his article 'The United States and Latin America: Ending the Hegemonic Presumption', *Foreign Affairs*, Vol.55 No.1. October 1976, pp.199-213.

35 *Izvestiya*, 7 August 1992.

36 *Op. cit.*, 'Towards a...'

37 John P. Vloyantes *Silk Glove Hegemony Finnish-Soviet Relations 1944-1974. A case study of the theory of the soft sphere of influence* (Kent State University Press, Kent, OH, 1975), p.3.

38 BBC, *SWB* SU/1629 B/1 5 March 1993.

39 See the article by Peter Reddaway in *The Independent*, 12 January 1993.

40 See George Maude *The Finnish Dilemma: Neutrality in the Shadow of Power* (OUP, London, 1976), for an analysis of Finnish foreign policy during the Cold War.
41 Cole Blasier *The Hovering Giant: U.S. responses to revolutionary change in Latin America 1910-1985*, rev. ed., (University of Pittsburgh Press, Pittsburgh, 1985); Walter Lafeber *Inevitable revolutions: the United States in Central America* (Norton, New York, 1983). Lafeber notes that between 1898 and 1920, the US intervened in Central America 20 times, p.11; Jenny Pearce, *Under the Eagle US intervention in Central America and the Caribbean* (Latin American Bureau, London, 1982), updated edition.
42 *Krasnaya Zvezda*, 20 February 1993. Karaganov outlines a policy for the creation of a Russian sphere of influence in greater detail in his article 'Problemy zashchity interesov rossiskogo naseleniya' in *Diplomatickesky Vestnik*, No. 21-22, 15-30 November 1992, pp.43-45.
43 *Rossiskaya Gazeta*, 12 February 1993.
44 *Rossiskaya Gazeta*, 23 May 1992. The treaty was signed by Russia, Armenia, Kyrgyzstan, Tajikistan, Kazakhstan, and Uzbekistan.
45 By March 1993, Kyrgyzstan, Armenia and Tajikistan had ratified the treaty See *RFE/RL News Briefs*, 15-19 March 1993, p.5.
46 *Izvestiya*, 9 July 1992. See also the interview with Shaposhnikov in BBC, *SWB* SU/1431 C4/1, 13 July 1992.
47 See the articles by Suzanne Crowe on peacekeeping in the CIS in *RFE/RL Research Report*, Vol. 1, No.37, 18 September 1992.
48 See the debate between Francis Fukuyama and Sergey Stankevich in which Fukuyama argues that Russia should redefine its national interest so that it excludes concern for the Russian diaspora in the 'near abroad' in *Nezavisimaya Gazeta*, 16 October 1992 and 6 November 1992.
49 BBC, *SWB* SU/1557 A1/1, 7 December 1992.
50 *Izvestiya*, 1 July 1992.
51 In an interview in *Moscow News*, No.23, 7-14 June 1992, p.14, Kozyrev rejected border changes. However, he spoke of the possibility of border changes in *Le Monde*, 7-8 June 1992.
52 See the interviews with Shelov-Kovedaev in *FBIS SOV 92 064*, 2 April 1992, p.22-23 and BBC, *SWB* SU/1496 A1/1, 26 September 1992.
53 BBC, *SWB* SU/1413 C2/2, 22 June 1992. An article in *Nezavismaya Gazeta* on 21 May 1992 contrasted the approaches of Rutskoy and Kozyrev over policy towards the CIS. It was reported in July 1992 that Rutskoy had called for Kozyrev's dismissal, *Financial Times*, 18 July 1992.
54 For Stankevich's views see for example *Nezavisimaya Gazeta*, 27 March 1992 and *Rossiskaya Gazeta*, 23 June 1992.
55 Ambartsumov includes not just the Russian diaspora and Russophones, but all those who identify with Russia. He speaks of 'even those who do not know Russian but look to Russia with hope', *Narodny Deputat*, No.16,

1992, p.17. Sergey Karaganov argues that Russia should assume responsibility for the 70 million former Soviet citizens who live outside the borders of their former Soviet republic, in *Krasnaya Zvezda*, 20 February 1993. See also 'Problemy zashchity interesov rossiskogo naseleniya' in *Diplomatickesky Vestnik*, No. 21-22, 15-30 November 1992, pp.43-45.

56 See the article by Rutskoy on Ukraine in *Rossiskaya Gazeta*, 20 May 1992.

57 See the discussion below.

58 *Le Monde*, 7-8 June 1992.

59 *The Independent*, 17 March 1993.

60 *Nezavisimaya Gazeta*, 28 March 1992. See also *Rossiskaya Gazeta*, 23 June 1992, in which he argues that Russia should use force to protect Russians in Georgia, Latvia, Estonia and Moldova.

61 BBC, *SWB* SU/1597, A1/3h 4, 27 January 1993.

62 *Nezavisimaya Gazeta*, 10 December 1992.

63 *FBIS SOV 92* 245, 21 December 1992, p.4.

64 *Krasnaya Zvezda*, 28 October 1992.

65 BBC, *SWB* SU/1641 B/1, 19 March 1993.

66 *Ibid.*

67 BBC, *SWB* SU/1627 i, 3 March 1993.

68 See Alan H Smith 'Economic Factors Affecting Soviet East European Relations in the 1980s' in Karen Dawisha and Philip Hanson eds. *Soviet East European Dilemmas: Coercion, Competition and Consent* (Heinemann, London, 1981), pp.108-133. See also the chapters by Paul Marer and John P Hardt in Sarah Meiklejohn Terry ed. *Soviet Policy in Eastern Europe* (Yale University Press, New Haven, 1984).

69 See Rutskoy's interview in *Der Spiegel*, 26 October 1992, pp.208 and 214.

70 *Komsomolskaya Pravda*, 14 July 1992.

71 BBC, *SWB* SU/1414 B/1, 23 June 1992.

72 BBC, *SWB* SU/1636 C1/7, 13 March 1993.

73 *FBIS SOV 92* 155, 11 August 1992 p.6.

THE BALTIC STATES

Russia probably puts its relations with the three Baltic states into a slightly different category than its relations with the rest of the former Soviet Union: it is probably more prepared to accept their rights to independence than those of the other ex-Soviet states. This is because of the independence that was enjoyed by these states in the inter-war period, and because their accession to the Soviet Union was never accepted *de jure* by the major Western states.

The Russian Federation recognised the declarations of independence made by Estonia, Latvia and Lithuania in August 1991 in the aftermath of the failed *putsch* in Moscow, and independence became a reality in September 1991, when the USSR recognised these states. The Soviet government then commenced a range of negotiations with the Baltic states, the most important of which comprised the withdrawal of the USSR armed forces from the three nations. When the USSR ceased to exist in December 1991, the Russian Federation replaced it as the negotiating partner of the Baltic states, and assumed full jurisdiction over the USSR armed forces in the Baltic states in a presidential decree issued in April 1992, which placed all ex-USSR armed forces outside the Russian Federation under Russian jurisdiction.

Relations between Moscow and the Baltic states have failed to develop smoothly since the break up of the Soviet Union, remaining at best cool. The Baltic states are wary of Moscow, suspecting that it views the states as part of a Russian sphere of influence, which in fact several Russian military officials do. In his critique of the Russian General Staff's proposed military doctrine, Rodionov argues that both an outlet to the Baltic seas and free access to Baltic ports are in Russia's interests. Rodionov argues that the stationing of the armed forces of any third power in the Baltic states, along with entrance into any anti-Russian military bloc by these states would run counter to Russian interests. In addition, he calls for the civil rights of the Russian population in these states to be guaranteed.[1]

Krasnaya Zvezda in October 1992 also examined Russian views of the role of the Baltic states.[2] In this discussion Lieutenant General

Aleksey Gulko, the deputy chief of the Main Directorate of the Russian Armed Forces, argued that the Baltic states are a zone of vital Russian interest. He likened Russian interest in the Baltic states to the US interest in the Persian Gulf states. In the same discussion, Iona Andronov, the deputy chairman of the Russian Supreme Soviet Committee of International Affairs and Foreign Economic Affairs, argued that 'our radar tracking complexes providing early warning of a nuclear attack are located in the Baltics. And if we lose them, all of the northeastern part of Russia will be open to missile attack. Russia will have to invest billions of roubles to restore this highly important system that provides for security.'

Andronov's views are shared by one of his fiercest opponents, the former first deputy foreign minister, Fedor Shelov Kovedaev, who argued that these early warning systems should be preserved after the withdrawal of Russian forces from the Baltic states. He proposed that they be jointly manned. In contrast to Andronov however, Shelov Kovedaev felt that the maintenance of these bases should be temporary until new ones are built elsewhere, presumably in Russia.[3]

In June 1992, the Lithuanian defence minister, Audrius Butkevicius, claimed that the former head of the now defunct CIS border guard troops, Colonel General Ilya Kalininchenko, informed him that 'the Polish Lithuanian border is seen as our [Russian] border and our soldiers are there to defend the interests of Russia.'[4]

There is therefore a clear Russian strategic interest in the Baltic region, and it is extremely difficult to see how these interests can be pursued without intruding on the sovereignty of these states. Gulko's analogy with the relationship between the US and the Persian Gulf states is misleading as the Gulf states currently desire a close security relationship with the US, whom they see as their principal source of protection. The leaderships of Estonia, Latvia and Lithuania instead see Russia as the most likely threat to their security, rather than as a protector.

Two main issues have dominated Russo-Baltic relations since 1991. These have been firstly the problems surrounding the withdrawal of Russian military forces from the three states, and secondly Moscow's concern over the position of the Russian communities in Estonia, Latvia and Lithuania.

The withdrawal of Russian military forces

The withdrawal of Russian military forces from the Baltic states has been a source of considerable friction between the Russia and the Baltic states. The Baltic states felt that it would become easier to reach formal agreements with Moscow on troop withdrawal after August 1991. Formal agreements have not so far materialised, although withdrawals have been taking place.

Estimates of the numbers of Russian forces in the three Baltic states vary. In 1990 unofficial estimates claimed that there were about 200 000 soldiers in Estonia, 300 000 in Latvia and 100 000 in Lithuania. In 1992 estimates of the total number of forces in all three states varied between 100 000 and 150 000. The numbers of troops stationed in each country also vary. A Swedish government study published in mid-1992 claimed the following force levels: Estonia 23 000; Latvia 48 000; Lithuania 43 000. The US State Department said in October 1992 that Russia had withdrawn 40 per cent of its forces from the Baltic states, leaving 9000 in Estonia, 24 500 in Lithuania and 44 500 in Latvia. Figures released in 1993 indicate that forces have been further reduced. Russian sources state that 5900 Russian soldiers are deployed in Estonia. The Latvian defence ministry claims that there are still 681 Russian troop units in Latvia totalling about 27 000 men (these figures have been challenged by Russian military sources). Lithuanian sources assert that there are about 14 000 Soviet troops in Lithuania.

The main obstacle to formal withdrawal agreements between Moscow and its Baltic partners lies in an inability to reach common agreement on withdrawal deadlines. The Baltic states have argued for all forces to be pulled out by the summer of 1993, but Russian military authorities have rejected this, arguing that the housing requirements for Russian forces mean that withdrawal cannot be completed until later in the decade. The years 1997 and 1999 have often been given by Russian military authorities as likely withdrawal dates. Apparent progress was made in the summer of 1992, when Yeltsin, in response to pressure from the US and Germany said that a withdrawal schedule would be drawn up for 1992 and 1993. At the CSCE meeting in Helsinki in July 1992, Russia effectively committed itself to an early withdrawal from the Baltic states (although no deadline was given).

In August 1992, however, Kozyrev met with the three Baltic foreign ministers in Moscow, and proposed that Russian forces could be withdrawn by 1994 provided several political conditions were met. These comprised granting legal status to the Russian armed forces in the interim period; allowing Russia to have temporary bases in the Baltic states; dropping compensation claims for damage done by USSR armed forces since 1940; help constructing housing in Russia for departing forces; to guarantee transit rights for military freight to Kaliningrad; to provide compensation for land and property vacated by Russian forces; to guarantee social security and human rights for Soviet officers who have retired to the Baltics; to alter laws that violated the rights of the Russian speaking population; to drop territorial claims against Russia.

These claims were unacceptable and were probably so designed by Moscow. The demand for bases is unlikely ever to be accepted by the Baltic states as they see it as a violation of their sovereignty, that could be used as a pretext for military intervention by Russia. All three Baltic states remember the how the USSR demanded and obtained military bases in September and October 1939, and how this was followed in 1940 by the incorporation of Estonia, Latvia and Lithuania into the Soviet Union. The demand that these states alter their citizenship laws to secure an early withdrawal of forces intrudes into internal affairs, and the request that the Baltic states drop compensation for environmental damage caused by Soviet forces since 1940 while simultaneously paying compensation to Russia for military facilities vacated, would seem to be designed as an offer that could only be rejected. This would then justify Moscow retaining forces after 1994 and prolonging negotiations on troop withdrawal.

Some progress was made in Russo-Lithuanian withdrawal negotiations in September 1992, when Moscow and Vilnius agreed that Russian forces would be withdrawn by September 1993. Similar agreements were not reached with Tallinn or Riga, and so have led to the belief that Moscow may be trying to drive a wedge between the Baltic states.

Lithuania is strategically less important than either Latvia or Estonia to Russia, as it contains no strategic facilities, and with the exception of the Kaliningrad oblast, has no border with Russia. The likelihood of a durable close relationship between Moscow and Minsk will give Moscow access to Lithuania. By retaining forces in Kaliningrad, Moscow also ensures that it will still able to project its influence in this region of the Baltic. Russia's leaders may also gamble that Lithuania's relations with Poland will remain cool, in the hope that this may encourage Vilnius to look towards Moscow. Its Russian population is also much smaller than its counterparts in Latvia and Estonia, and so Moscow probably feels more confident in removing its forces from Lithuania.

The linkage of Russian force withdrawals with the status of the Russian communities in the Baltic states is potentially ominous. As the Russian populations in the Baltic states are likely to remain there, this could give Moscow a permanent excuse to express concern about the status of these communities, and demand that Russian forces protect them. Both the Russian military and political leadership have already voiced such concerns.

In June 1992 the Russian defence minister, Pavel Grachev, addressed Russian forces in the Baltic states, Transcaucasia and Moldova and warned that 'attempts were being made to draw the army into conflicts ever more frequently. Servicemen and civilians are dying at the hands of extremists. Sooner or later it will be necessary to respond to all this. In conditions of civil chaos, clashes and reprisals, only the army can save thousands of lives...and defend what is sacred.' Grachev then spoke of the hostility being shown to 'the Russophone population, servicemen of the Russian army and members of servicemen's families.'[5] In October 1992, Yeltsin declared that the withdrawal of Russian forces from the Baltic states was being suspended. The decision to halt withdrawal was connected to deep concern for the numerous violations of the rights of the Russian speaking population in these republics.[6]

A letter sent by Yeltsin to the UN Secretary General in November 1992, claimed that human rights in the Baltic states were being violated on a 'massive scale'. Yeltsin confirmed that Russia would withdraw its forces and said that withdrawal would be 'resumed and completed according to tight, realistic deadlines after the signing of interstate agreements.' The next paragraph of the letter declared 'that at the same time the further development of Russia's relations with the Baltic states will to a large extent depend on the situation of the Russian speaking population in them'.[7] One of the most dramatic statements by a Russian political figure came from foreign minister Andrey Kozyrev in March 1993. He threatened that a new Yugoslavia could erupt in the Baltic states, which would require the deployment of a vast number of peacekeeping troops (presumably Russian).[8]

It is true that forces are continuing to withdraw despite Yeltsin's decree, and that eventually full withdrawal may be reached despite the lack of formal interstate agreements. However, the lack of these agreements could provoke a situation in which a future Russian leadership might argue that there is no legal document confirming that it has withdrawn from the Baltics, and so no agreement is being violated if forces re-enter either to protect the Russian population or for strategic reasons. The existence of a legal vacuum may also create uncertainty in the minds of Baltic policymakers about the wisdom of shifting too far from Moscow in their foreign and security policy orientation.

Russian military observers express concern that the Baltic states are veering towards NATO. In September 1992 in *Krasnaya Zvezda* the Russian Navy warned of the possibility of NATO states cooperating militarily with the Baltic states. *Krasnaya Zvezda* commented:

> The question of creating military bases on the pretext of protecting Baltic democracy will be worked out. First they will raise the question of refuelling warships, from this they will progress to the partial use of ports for military purposes, and this will most likely be followed by a request to set up Western states' naval bases, which will be in direct proximity to Russian borders.[9]

In an interview with the Finnish newspaper *Helsingin Sanomat* in February 1993, Lieutenant General Fyodor Melnichuk, the deputy commander of the Northwestern group of forces, said that he regarded NATO to some degree as a an enemy of Russia, and that Russian military bases should remain in Latvia for some decades.[10]

In March 1993 it was reported in Lithuania that the US Navy had invited Lithuania, Estonia and Latvia to participate in the NATO naval exercise, BALTIC OPERATION 93, in June 1993.[11] Any form of participation, no matter how limited, will be viewed by Moscow as challenge to its position in the Baltic. Military disapproval of the Baltic states' preference to see the West as a security partner is likely to result in a semi-permanent coolness in relations between Moscow and the three states.

Despite the withdrawals that are taking place, there have been intrusions on the sovereignty of the Baltic states by Russian forces stationed there. Latvia claims that Russian troops have been sent into Latvia without Latvian authorisation, and at the beginning of March 1993, the Latvian foreign minister, Georgs Andrejevs, said that Russian military aircraft had violated Latvian airspace 222 times in January and February 1993. He also claimed that Russian military transport in Latvia has often been moved about the country without permission. Similar incidents have occurred constantly in 1992 and 1993. In February 1993, the Estonian authorities claimed that a Russian naval transport vessel arrived at Paltiski without permission. In January the Lithuanian defence ministry claimed that permission had been granted for 207 Russian soldiers to enter the country in order to help with the withdrawal of the 7th Airborne division: however, 929 soldiers actually entered Lithuania.[12]

In October 1992 the Russian deputy defence minister, Boris Gromov, visited Russian troops in Latvia without informing the Latvian authorities of his visit, so violating Latvian sovereignty. Gromov stated that withdrawal from the Baltic states would take seven to eight years and would not start before 1995, so once again pushing the final departure date further and further into the future.[13] Unannounced visits by Russian military officials to ex-Soviet states happen frequently, and indicates the Russian military's disrespect for the sovereignty of the states of the 'near abroad'.

In 1992, in Estonia, there were several armed clashes between Estonian security forces and Russian troops. It is impossible to determine who provoked these incidents, but while Russian forces remain, there is always the possibility that such incidents could occur and be used as a pretext by Russia for intervention in the Baltic states.[14]

It is in Latvia, where the most important military facilities are located, that Russian attention is likely to be concentrated. Riga is the headquarters of the Northwestern group of forces (the former Baltic military district) and the site where the most important strategic facilities are located. Three facilities are particularly important: the phased array radar at Skrunde; the laser detection centre in Rinda, Ventspils; and the naval bases in Liepaja. Russia is likely to withdraw from Latvia after any withdrawal from Lithuania and Estonia.[15]

The nationality issue in the Baltics

As already noted, the nationality issue in the Baltic states has been linked by Russian officials with the presence of Russian troops. A significant proportion of Russian settlers in the Baltic states are retired Soviet officers, and the Estonian defence minister described those retirees as a threat to national security. In Latvia, organisations of both serving and retired officers have become politically active and developed links with hardline organisations in Russia such as the Union of Officers and the National Salvation Front. If a hardline regime were to come to power in Russia, these organisations could then mount a significant challenge to the governments in the Baltic states.

Russia objects to the citizenship law that came into force in Estonia in February 1992 and to the guidelines on a citizenship law adopted by the Latvian parliament in October 1991 on the grounds that it denies the Russian communities in these states the right to citizenship. In October 1992, Sergey Stankevich wrote to the Council of Europe complaining that 900 000 ethnic Russians in Latvia, and 600 000 in Estonia, had been deprived of the possibility of becoming loyal citizens of those countries. Moves by Estonia to moderate some aspects of its citizenship laws have been rejected as cosmetic by Moscow, and only a major change granting immediate citizenship is likely to be accepted. Moscow may also demand that the Russian communities be permitted dual citizenship. The existence of Russian communities in all three states gives Moscow a permanent lever in the internal affairs of the Baltic states. This factor, plus Russian perceptions of a drift towards NATO and concern over the loss of strategic bases in the region, means that pressure from Moscow is likely to be a constant feature of Russia's relations with Estonia, Latvia and Lithuania.

1 Speech by Igor Rodionov at the conference on Russian military doctrine held in Moscow, 27-30 May 1992. My copy of the speech was obtained from a private source. A version of Rodionov's speech also appeared in a special number of *Voennaya Mysl'* in July 1992.
2 *Krasnaya Zvezda*, 10 October 1992.
3 *Izvestiya*, 22 August 1992.
4 *Financial Times*, 15 June 1992.
5 BBC, *SWB* SU/1421 i, 1 July 1992.
6 BBC, *SWB* SU/1526 A2/1, 31 October 1992.
7 BBC, *SWB* SU/1533 A2/1-9, November 1992.
8 *The Independent*, 17 March 1993.
9 *Krasnaya Zvezda*, 18 September 1992. A more dramatic view of NATO penetration of the Baltic states appeared in *Krasnaya Zvezda*, 5 March 1992.
10 *Helsingin Sanomat*, 4 February 1993, in *FBIS USR* 93 034, 19 March 1993, p.60.
11 BBC, *SWB* SU/1635 A2/1, 12 March 1993.
12 The weekly Tallinn based English language newspaper *The Baltic Independent* runs a column entitled 'Troop Watch', which details incidents relating to Russian forces in the Baltic states.
13 Dzintra Bungs 'Russian Troop Withdrawal from Latvia; An Update', *RFE/RL Research Report*, Vol.1, No.49, 11 December 1992, p.29.
14 In April 1992, the Lithuanian authorities arrested Colonel Ivan Chernykh, Commander of the coast defence division of the Baltic Fleet, who had supported the August 1991 coup. This led to friction with the local Russian military authorities and with Moscow. Rutskoy allegedly sent Landsbergis a threatening telegram demanding the release of

Chernykh. See BBC, *SWB* SU/1352 A2/1-2, 10 April 1992, and BBC, *SWB* SU/1353 A2/Z, 11 April 1992.

15 Note that Sergey Zotov, the leader of the Russian delegation negotiating troop withdrawals with Latvia, claimed in October that Latvia had allowed Russia to maintain the Skrunde facility after Russian forces had finally withdrawn. This was denied by his Latvian opposite number Janis Dinevics. Zotov is reported to have expressed regret about Russia's decision to recognise the independence of the Baltic states. See Dzintra Bungs 'Russian Troop Withdrawal from Latvia; An Update', *RFE/RL Research Report*, Vol.1 No.49, 11 December 1992, p.29-30.

THE CORE STATES

The core of the Russian security zone, apart from the Russian Federation, consists of Ukraine and Belarus (who were, along with Russia, the founder members of the CIS), and Kazakhstan. In late 1990 these four union republics (as they then were) were negotiating the formation of a quadripartite confederation that would have effectively stood as an alternative to the new union treaty that Gorbachev was endeavouring to work out with the republics. The Russian Federation, Ukraine, Belarus and Kazakhastan made up the core of the Soviet Union, comprising 91.96 per cent of the area of the USSR, 78.59 per cent of the Soviet population, and about 85 per cent of the Net Material Product of the Soviet Union.[1] The Soviet strategic nuclear arsenal was also deployed in these republics. Politically, economically and militarily, these union republics were the most important component parts of the Soviet Union.

It is therefore quite logical that Russian thinking continues to see these four states as important. In 1990, Alexander Solzhenitsyn advocated a Pan-Russian union comprising Russia, Ukraine, Belarus and the Russian regions of northern Kazakhstan. The desire for such a union is probably strongly held by many in the foreign and security policy establishment in Moscow.

The Civic Union's programme regards the interrelationship between the four states as crucial:

> Ukraine, Belarusia and Kazakhstan are Russia's main partners in maintaining stability in the post Soviet geo-political space, in containing and regulating conflicts, in ensuring human rights, and in developing coordinated economic mechanisms of cooperation. After the non-nuclear status of these states becomes a fact, Russia is prepared to assume those responsibilities in the sphere of joint defence which may be desirable to them.

Yury Nazarkin, formerly a disarmament specialist in the Russian foreign ministry, and now a member of the Russian Security Council, echoes this thinking, arguing that Ukraine, Belarus and Kazakhstan are

Russia's natural allies, being linked both economically and psychologically.[2]

The Slavic identity of three of these states (Russians also comprise 37.8 per cent of Kazakhstan's population, and Ukrainians 5.4 per cent) is seen by Russia as providing the natural basis for a close union. Galina Starovoitova, who was formerly an adviser to Yeltsin on ethnic issues, favoured the idea of a Slavic Union. The Russian armed forces, as it seeks a new ideological identity after the collapse of Marxism Leninism, is likely to look to both Russian nationalism and Pan-Slavism as a source of identity. In May 1992, *Krasnaya Zvezda* devoted considerable attention to the festival of Slavic literature and culture that coincided with the day of St Cyril and St Methodius which became a public holiday in Russia in 1991. *Krasnaya Zvezda* regarded the festival as an indication of the 'rebirth of the spirit of Slavdom, as an important condition of strengthening stability in the world.'[3]

Belarus

Russia's relations with Belarus are probably viewed by Moscow as a model for the type of relations that it would desire with all states from the 'near abroad'. Minsk's foreign policy is largely oriented towards Moscow, and the government in Minsk has so far shown little inclination to shift away from this orientation. It appears unlikely that Minsk will be tempted to follow the Ukrainian path and adopt a stance that is more challenging of Moscow, as Belarusian nationalism is much less assertive than its Ukrainian counterpart and pro-Moscow political forces play a much more influential role in Belarus than in Ukraine. It is probably not an exaggeration to say that Belarus did not even seek independence in August 1991 when the Soviet Union passed into the final phase of its disintegration. It was more a case of independence being thrust upon Belarus.

This is not to say that Belarusian policy has obediently followed Moscow since the formation of the CIS. In March 1992, the Belarusian Supreme Soviet voted in favour of establishing Belarusian armed forces, and Belarus has subsequently proceeded with the creation of its own army.

Belarus' refusal to sign the Tashkent collective security agreement in May 1992 was a blow to Moscow's hopes of establishing an alliance embracing all members of the CIS. As neither Ukraine, Belarus or Moldova signed the treaty, Russia was the sole European signatory at Tashkent. The Belarusian leadership cited its adherence to neutrality in its July 1990 declaration of sovereignty as the reason for non-participation in the Tashkent agreement, and this refusal to sign the agreement is the greatest demonstration of independence from Moscow by Minsk. It does not, however, signify a major rupture with Moscow. In early May 1992, the chairman of the Belarusian Supreme Soviet, Stanislav Shushkevich, denied that there were any 'Russian imperial positions that we Belarusians must do battle with'. In general, Belarus has been an enthusiastic supporter of integration within the CIS, and in the military sphere Belarus has been extremely cooperative with Moscow. Tactical nuclear weapons were withdrawn from Belarus without interruption (in contrast to Ukraine) in May 1992, and Belarus has transferred the jurisdiction of the strategic nuclear weapons deployed on its territory to Russia.

The foundation of Russo-Belarusian relations is the wide ranging network of political, economic and military agreements between the two states that were signed between their respective prime ministers in July 1992. The Belarusian prime minister, Vyacheslav Kebich, described the agreements as providing a comprehensive union between the two states. The Russian prime minister, Egor Gaidar, said that the agreements were a step towards a confederation, although Kebich distanced himself slightly from this description, referring to 'small steps'. Kebich did, however, draw special attention to the military cooperation agreement reached.[4] The Belarusian defence minister, Pavel Kozlovsky, commented that this agreement does not constitute an alliance, but that it does lay the basis for close military cooperation between Moscow and Minsk.[5]

These agreements may not constitute a formal alliance, but they do establish an extremely close linkage that appears to have more substance than the insistence of Belarusian leaders of their state's neutrality. Belarus' military doctrine confirms Minsk's neutrality, but reserves the right to seek the assistance of other states if a threat to Belarusian security arises. Belarus' most probable partner in such a situation would be Russia. Minsk is already dependent on Russia in the military sphere, and is unlikely to be able to reduce this dependence in the near term. In June 1992 it was agreed that Russia would finance Belarus' defence enterprises, and in December 1992 it was revealed that 47 per cent of the personnel in the armed forces were Russian citizens. Belarus is genuine in its desire to develop close economic and political ties with all European states, but its level of military dependency on Russia is likely to give a strong pro-Moscow slant to Belarusian neutrality for some time to come.

There are, however, challenges to this policy in line in Belarus. Shushkevich is reportedly less enthusiastic about the July 1992 agreements than Kebich, who appears more pro-Russian than the Supreme Soviet chairman.[6] Belarusian politics is still largely dominated by those who held sway before August 1991. The Belarusian Popular Front (BPF), if it came to power, would pursue a more independent foreign policy and move away from the Moscow line favoured by Kebich, and the chairman of the BPF, Xenon Pozdniak, views Germany as Belarus' natural partner in Europe.[7]

Belarus' current foreign policy stance suits Moscow perfectly, and provides Russia with its sole means of direct access to Central Europe now that Ukraine is determined to avoid being closely tied to Moscow. Too enthusiastic a westward drift in Belarusian policy would create discomfort in Moscow. Belarus' relationship with Poland in 1991 was cool, although it improved in 1992 with the signing of several agreements including a treaty on good neighbourly relations and cooperation in June, when Shushkevich visited Warsaw. Russia would prefer to see the maintenance of the *status quo* in Belarusian foreign policy, and the decision of the Belarusian parliament to sign the Tashkent collective security agreement in April 1993 was thus a success for Moscow. It is interesting that the foreign minister, Petr Kravchenko remarked that Belarus' relations with Russia should be modelled on Soviet Finnish relations from 1948 to 1991. This virtually amounts to a desire for 'Finlandisation'.[8]

Ukraine

Russia's relations with Ukraine since independence have frequently touched raw nerves in Moscow, and have provided the toughest test for Russia's claims that it is pursuing a non-imperial policy towards the 'near abroad'. Russia has found it difficult to reconcile itself to the emergence of an independent Ukraine. Indeed, it is more accurate to argue that Russia does not and will not fully accept Ukrainian independence. The perception that the Russian state originated in Ukraine evokes strong feelings in Russia, and this sentiment is unlikely to fade. Russia hoped that the CIS would provide a framework for close Russo-Ukrainian cooperation, and Moscow has been disappointed by Ukraine's lack of interest in cooperation and by its desire to see the CIS more as a means of divorcing itself from remaining structures of the former Soviet Union rather than of cooperation.

Ukraine has been determined to build its own armed forces since Kiev declared independence in August 1991. The Ukrainian draft military doctrine identifies no specific state as a threat, but 'it regards as a potential enemy all states that have territorial claims against Ukraine, interfere in its internal affairs, form or join alliances directed against the political, economic and military interests of Ukraine.' Under the terms of this doctrine, the state that comes closest to being a threat is the Russian Federation. The government of the Russian Federation has not raised any territorial claims against Ukraine, but it is quite possible that the status of Crimea could become an object of dispute between Kiev and Moscow.

In May 1992, the Russian Supreme Soviet adopted a draft resolution ruling that the transfer of Crimea from Russia to Ukraine by Nikita Khrushchev in 1954 was illegal, and calls for interstate talks between Russia and Crimea to determine the status of Crimea. This is not a formal territorial demand by the Russian government, but if the parliament is able to make such a claim, then so of course can the government. In April 1992, Russian vice president Alexander Rutskoy visited Crimea apparently without seeking the consent of the Ukrainian authorities, and stated that 'common sense prompts: the Crimea should be part of Russia and sign the Federative Agreement', and spoke in favour of a referendum, saying that 'if the peoples of

Crimea decide to join Russia, the Republic of Crimea will be perfectly able to exist as part of the Russian Federation.' Rutskoy's actions hardly denote respect for Ukrainian sovereignty, and in Ukrainian eyes undermine the agreement that he reached with Ukraine's leaders in August 1991 confirming the November 1990 Russo-Ukrainian treaty which accepts existing borders as inviolable.

When a member of the Russian executive such as Rutskoy makes these assessments, it is likely that they fuel the Ukrainian perception of Russia as an imperial state that views Ukraine as part of a Russian sphere of influence.   Rutskoy wrote a very emotive article in *Rossiskaya Gazeta* in May 1992, in which he bitterly attacked the Ukrainian leadership for poisoning Russo-Ukrainian relations. He has the belief that it is natural for Ukraine and Russia to act as one, and gives the impression that he regards Ukrainian independence as an unnatural phenomenon.   He states that the 'Ukrainian separatists' efforts to break completely with Russia, to detach themselves from the Russian political space will lead to the formation of a permanent bed of ethnic religious conflict in Ukraine...But everyone must think hard before relations take an abrupt downturn. Over more than 1000 years Russia has demonstrated its viability and ability to 'stand up and rise up'.   But what will become of Ukrainian statehood, which is taking its first steps, statehood which certain people are pushing onto the path of confrontation and expansion.'?[9]

Elsewhere in his article Rutskoy cites figures demonstrating the interdependence of the Russian and Ukrainian economies. He writes that 'Russian industry depends on deliveries from Ukraine to the tune of 12 per cent and Ukraine on Russian deliveries to the tune of 67 per cent. The figures for raw materials and energy sources are still more eloquent. Deliveries from Russia entirely determine the capability of the Ukrainian construction industry, mining industry, heavy industry, all energy intensive sectors and agricultural production. We are so interlinked that we cannot be untied.' Given Rutskoy's disapproval of the policies pursued by the Kiev leadership, and his advocacy that Russia should impose economic sanctions against states from the 'near abroad', then Ukrainian leaders may well see Rutskoy's comments on economic interdependence as an implied threat.

Rutskoy's views on Ukraine are not untypical in Russia. In December 1992, Yeltsin's political adviser, Sergey Stankevich, was interviewed in *Holos Ukrainy* and criticised the existence of extreme stereotypes in Ukraine and Russia. He condemned the Ukrainian notion of defining independence by a policy of distance from Russia; but his remarks on Russian thinking would appear to justify Ukrainian perceptions of an imperial threat from Moscow:

> We have a complex of attitudes towards Ukraine as though it was a temporarily lost territory. It is as though because of various circumstances there was a misunderstanding, a natural disaster, or a traffic accident on our historical road, and all one has to do to is set it right or repair it. By the method of pressure and exigency or using economic levers or waiting while Ukraine tries to live independently, realises this is impossible, and like a ripe fruit, falls at Russia's feet. It is as though one needs only a little patience and a little economic pressure. There are also extreme views—to return it by force. And this too is not simple a stereotype of mass consciousness. Such an attitude is noticeable in Russia at all levels. It too must be abandoned.[10]

Ukrainian suspicions of Russian imperialism, which have been strongly fuelled by the dispute over Crimea and the division of the Black Sea Fleet, explain Ukraine's reluctance to cooperate too closely with the CIS. Ukraine refused to sign either the Tashkent collective security agreement or the CIS Charter, which President Leonid Kravchuk has likened to the implementation of the 1922 union treaty that established the USSR.[11] This comparison is exaggerated, but it emphasises Ukraine's aversion to being closely linked to cooperative structures amongst ex-Soviet states.

Russia appears to accept that Ukraine will never be an enthusiastic member of the CIS, and so since the latter half of 1992, has moved towards trying to build a close bilateral relationship with Ukraine outside of the CIS framework. It has been argued in Russia that Moscow should instead try to consolidate the CIS around Russia, Belarus and Kazakhstan and develop ties with Ukraine on a bilateral basis.[12] The summit held between Yeltsin and Kravchuk at

Dagomyys in June 1992, marked the beginning of this process, when it was agreed that a Russo-Ukrainian friendship and cooperation treaty would be negotiated. From the draft treaty presented by Russia it is evident that Moscow envisages a degree of security cooperation that Kiev views as hegemonic. The treaty apparently assumes that Russia and Ukraine would be allies, defending a common 'regional military strategic space'. Russia's armed forces would have the right to use 'installations and territories in Ukraine' (Articles seven and eight).[13]

At the round table discussion on Russian security interests organised by *Krasnaya Zvezda* in October 1992, Gulko argued that Ukraine could be the partner of Russia in the way that Britain partners the US.[14] Moscow's problem is that Kiev simply does not desire such a close relationship, which it feels would be dominated by Moscow.

Ukraine's continued ambiguity over ratifying START 1 and joining the nuclear non-proliferation regime, plus its wish to assume greater control over nuclear weapons stationed in the country, are prompted by the desire to use its share of the former USSR nuclear arsenal as a lever to force the West to take note of Ukraine's security concerns. Kiev's nuclear policy demonstrates its continued suspicion of Moscow, and its lack of interest in developing close ties with Russia. Kiev's negative response to Yeltsin's proposal that the UN grant Russia special rights as a peacekeeper on the territory of the former USSR was inevitable, and simply strengthened Ukrainian suspicions of Moscow.[15]

Ukraine's main strategic interest lies in reducing its dependence on Moscow. Throughout 1992 and 1993, Kiev has concentrated on improving its political, economic and military ties with its immediate western neighbours in Central Europe. A Polish-Ukrainian friendship and cooperation treaty was signed in May 1992, and the Polish prime minister, Hanna Suchocka, visited Ukraine in January 1993. This was followed by a visit from the Polish defence minister in February when a military cooperation agreement was signed. In general, Ukraine would like to develop closer ties with all the Visegrad states which it sees as stepping stones to closer ties with Western Europe. Ukraine has also sought close political ties with Hungary.[16]

This strategy has been a source of irritation in Moscow, with reports that Moscow has apparently been informing East European states not to develop too close a relationship with Ukraine. Stankevich warned Warsaw in early 1993 that Ukraine and Belarus lie within a Russian sphere of influence.[17] This warning confirms Russian sensitivity about the 'near abroad' falling under the influence of outside states. Ukraine presently remains heavily dependent on Moscow for energy supplies, and the dispute between Russia and Ukraine over gas prices in early 1993, and Russian problems in supplying oil to Ukraine, highlight Ukraine's dependence on Russia.[18]

Ukraine's agreement with Iran in February 1993 to purchase Iranian oil is indicative of Kiev's desire to reduce energy dependence on Russia.[19] In March 1993, the then first deputy prime minister, Ihor Yuknovsky, spoke of the possibility of Ukraine shipping Azerbaijani and Turkmen oil and gas from the Georgian port of Poti on the Black Sea (so bypassing Russia), and stated that Georgia was strategically important to Ukraine.[20] Kiev will therefore be concerned about Russian involvement in the Georgian conflict.

The Ukrainian military industrial complex (MIC) is also dependent on ties with its Russian counterpart; to the tune of 70 per cent according to Ukrainian defence minister Konstantyn Morozov.[21] There are no closed cycles of weapons production in Ukraine, and Kiev is now developing programmes to overcome this and reduce dependence on Russia by developing ties with new partners. Morozov declared that agreements had been signed with Poland, Hungary, Czechoslovakia and Bulgaria.[22]

If Ukraine is successful in reducing its dependence on Russia and is able to consolidate friendly relations with its western neighbours, then Russia's concerns about the drift of Ukraine away from its sphere of influence will grow. If Yeltsin is replaced by a more nationalist leader then the relationship between Kiev and Moscow will deteriorate, and as in the case of the Baltic states, Moscow is likely to accuse NATO of pulling Ukraine into its sphere of influence.[23] The most likely flashpoint in Russo-Ukrainian relations will be the status of Crimea, which has effectively been placed on the agenda by the Russian Supreme Soviet's ruling that the 1954 transfer was illegal. A

45

Russian threat to Ukraine could provide the West with the most serious challenge to security in Eastern Europe since the end of the Cold War, and make clear how seriously the West takes Ukrainian independence.

Kazakhstan and Central Asia

As discussed earlier, Kazakhstan is viewed by Moscow as one of its strategic partners in the CIS. Its size (it was the second largest union republic), the large number of Russians residing there (about 6.22 million, some 37.8 per cent of the population) the length of its frontier with Russia (7200 kilometres), its position between Russia and China and role as a Central Asian state, emphasise Kazakhstan's strategic importance in Russian eyes. This is reinforced by the fact that part of the former USSR's strategic arsenal is deployed on Kazakh territory.

Kazakhstan is potentially extremely vulnerable. As noted above, a substantial proportion of its population is Russian, and the Kazakh population is not much larger (39.7 per cent, that is 6.58 million). Most of the Russians live in the northern half of Kazakhstan, and many of them occupy important posts. It is possible that Kazakhstan could split in two, with the northern half being absorbed by Russia. It is also possible that ethnic conflict could erupt between the Russian and Kazakh communities, which would carry the danger of Russian intervention. This vulnerability explains the reaction of president Nursultan Nazarbaev to the Russian threat to demand the revision of borders with neighbouring states that sought to leave the Soviet Union in August 1991.[24] Kazakhstan's sense of insecurity is reinforced by the fact that it used to form part of the Russian Soviet Federated Socialist Republic, and did not acquire union republic status until 1936.

Nazarbaev has responded to this vulnerability by promoting Kazakhstan as a reliable ally of Russia, so giving Moscow no cause for concern about the policy course of Alma Ata. The Kazakh president regards Russia as a 'strategic partner',[25] and favours close integration within the CIS as the best means of ensuring stability both for Russo-Kazakh relations and the CIS.[26]

From the Russian perspective, Nazarbaev's current policy is ideal. In May 1992, Russia and Kazakhstan concluded a 25 year treaty of friendship and mutual cooperation, under the terms of which Russia will assist Kazakhstan in building its own armed forces. The treaty also provides for the joint use of military and space facilities. In strategic terms Russia and Kazakhstan see their two states as a single strategic zone: both states will promote economic cooperation in order to create a single economic zone and will grant each other MFN status. *Krasnaya Zvezda* regarded the treaty as establishing a defensive alliance.[27] A close relationship with Kazakhstan is an integral feature of the Eurasian element in Russian foreign policy strategy. To sign a treaty of such duration, indicates that Russia's interest in Kazakhstan is long term.

The conclusion of this treaty was quickly followed by treaties with other Central Asian states. A Russo-Uzbek treaty was signed in May, and a treaty with Kyrgyzstan followed in June. A Russo-Turkmen treaty was signed in July, and a treaty with Tajikistan has been delayed due to the conflict in that country. With the exception of the Kyrgyz president, Askar Akaev, all the leaderships in Central Asia are the former communist leaderships that opposed the break up of the old Soviet Union. Like Nazarbaev, they now look to close ties with Russia in place of the old Soviet Union. Their security interests coincide with Moscow's as they all fear the spread of Islamic fundamentalism from the regions to the south of Central Asia, and the network of treaties that Moscow has signed with these states, along with the Tashkent collective security treaty, emphasises Russia's interest in having these states as strategic allies. When the Russo-Uzbek treaty was signed in May, Uzbek president Islam Karimov was at pains to emphasise Russia's importance to the security of Central Asia. Karimov assessed Russia as guaranteeing 'stability and peace in our region and preserving the integrity of our frontiers'.

As long as former communist leaderships remain in power in Central Asia, they are likely to look to Moscow as a guarantor of their security. This coincides neatly with Moscow's desire to have friendly regimes in Central Asia. Russia has been assisting the Tajik government in Dushanbe in its fight with Islamic forces backed by Afghani *majuhedin*, and border troops from Russia and other CIS members have assumed responsibility for guarding the Tajik-Afghan border. In September 1992, the Russian foreign ministry warned that 'interference in Tajikistan would threaten the security not only of the Central Asian states but also of Russia'.[28] The security of the Russian population in Tajikistan has been one of the main concerns of the Russian leadership, and Kozyrev declared in October 1992 that the 'entire might of the Russian state is poised to defend human rights, including the rights of Russians and the Russian speaking population'.[29]

Russia has accordingly backed the Tajik government because of its fears of Islamic extremism penetrating Central Asia. The Tajik defence minister, Alexander Shishlyannikov (a Russian), who was appointed in early 1993, regards the 201st division as the guarantor of stability in Tajikistan.[30] It appears to be prepared to act as the 'security manager' in Central Asia to ensure that Russian influence is not diminished. The fear that the Russian populations there could become potential hostages to fundamentalist regimes is an important factor motivating Russia to maintain a presence. Alongside the interstate treaties concluded in 1992, Russia is assisting these states in the construction of their own armed forces.

However, although the Central Asian states have a mutual interest with Russia in opposing Islamic fundamentalism, their interests also diverge. The establishment of closer ties with states such as Turkey and Iran is a central feature of the foreign policy of most Central Asian states, and this may in the long term reduce Moscow's influence in the region and result in these states shifting their orientation away from Moscow. It has already been seen how several influential Russians are concerned about the growth of the influence of Turkey and other powers in Central Asia, and just as Russia is discomforted about the shift of Ukraine away from Moscow, it is likely to feel equally insecure if Central Asian states look southwards rather than northwards. From Moscow's perspective, the most serious potential problem is likely to be Kazakhstan. If Alma Ata turns away from Nazarbaev's current Russian policy, then it is increasingly likely that the Kazakh republic would split. Russia's interest in developing the armed forces of these states represents an attempt to maintain its role as the key actor in determining their security affairs.

Central Asia has been described as a 'time bomb' of potential ethnic conflicts and border disputes.[31] There is for example, fear of Uzbek expansionism in several other states. Ethnic conflict between Tajiks and Uzbeks in Tajikistan (Uzbeks comprise 23.5 per cent of the population) is seen as another threat to regional security. A survey published by the former USSR Academy of Sciences Institute of Geography in 1991 listed 20 potential ethnic and territorial disputes in Central Asia.[32] If territorial and ethnic conflicts spread, then Russia is likely to become more active in organising peacekeeping operations and proposing regional security regimes with substantial Russian underpinning.[33]

1 See the chart in *The Independent*, 30 August 1991.
2 *Krasnaya Zvezda*, 10 October 1992.
3 *Krasnaya Zvezda*, 22 May 1992.
4 *Nezavisimaya Gazeta*, 22 July 1992.
5 *Krasnaya Zvezda*, 22 July 1992.
6 *Nezavisimaya Gazeta*, 19 September 1992.
7 Kathleen Mihalisko 'The Outlook for Independent Belarus', *RFE/RL Research Report*, Vol.1, No.24, 12 June 1992, p.11.
8 BBC, *SWB* SU/1661 B/11, 13 April 1993.
9 *Rossiskaya Gazeta*, 20 May 1992.
10 *Holos Ukrainy*, 30 December 1992.
11 See Kravchuk's interview with the Israeli newspaper *Ha'aretz*, 15 January 1993, *FBIS USR* 93 011, 29 January 1993, p.46-47.
12 See Karaganov's article in *Krasnaya Zvezda*, 20 February 1993.
13 See John Lough 'The Place of the 'Near Abroad' in Russian Foreign Policy', *RFE/RL Research Report*, Vol.2, No.11, 12 March 1993 p.26.
14 *Krasnaya Zvezda*, 10 October 1992.

15 The Ukrainian foreign ministry saw Yeltsin's speech as 'a gross violation of international law, including the UN Charter and CSCE documents'. See *Ukrainian Business Agency Bulletin*, 15 March 1993, p.2.
16 *RFE/RL* Report Vol.2. No.16 pp.
17 *Financial Times*, 17 March 1993.
18 An article in *Nezavisimaya Gazeta*, 15 January 1993, stated that 70 per cent of Ukraine's economy oriented toward Russia. Ukrainian prime minister Leonid Kuchma commented in March 1993 that Russia may have delayed energy supplies because it was seeking Ukrainian political concessions over Sevastopol. See BBC, *SWB* SU/1645 C2/4, 24 March 1993.
19 BBC, *SWB* SU/1616 A1/4, 18 February 1993.
20 BBC, *SWB* SU/1630 B/13, 6 March 1993. Note that on 13 April 1993 Shevardnadze and Kravchuk signed a Georgian-Ukrainian friendship treaty, according to which, Georgia and Ukraine will both cooperate against a 'third force' presumably Russia, *Financial Times*, 14 April 1993.
21 *Nezavisimaya Gazeta*, 23 October 1992.
22 *Uradovy Kurier*, 4 December 1992.
23 An article in *Krasnaya Zvezda* in December 1992 expressed concern that NATO was taking advantage of the problems surrounding the BSF to expand its influence in the Black Sea region. See *Krasnaya Zzevda*, 24 December 1992.
24 Nazarbaev warned that border revision by Russia could lead to war. BBC, *SWB* SU/1162, B/14 28 August 1991.
25 *Sovetskaya Rossiya*, 13 February 1993 and *Krasnaya Zvezda*, 23 February 1993.
26 In March 1993, Nazarbaev sent Yeltsin a telegram with proposals for strengthening the CIS. See BBC, *SWB* SU/1647 B/2h 3, 26 March 1993.
27 *Krasnaya Zvezda*, 27 May 1992. Note also that joint Russo-Kazakh military exercises took place in October 1992. See *FBIS SOV* 92 207, 26 October 1992, p.2.
28 *RFE/RL Research Report*, Weekly Review, Vol.1, No.37, 18 September 1992, p.72. In his visit to Tajikistan in February 1993, Grachev said that the 201st division in Tajikistan should be bolstered because the region was strategically important to Moscow See *RFE/RL News Briefs* 8-12 February 1993, p.8

29 *RFE/RL Research Report*, Weekly Review, Vol 1, No.44, 6 November 1992, p.71.

30 *RFE/RL News Briefs*, 15-19 February 1993, p.8.

31 *Nezavisimaya Gazeta*, 25 December 1992.

32 *Moscow News*, No.11, 10-17 March 1991, pp.8-9

33 Some Russian foreign policy analysts contend that Russia should reduce its ties with Central Asia, arguing that Russia is a European rather than a Eurasian state. See Andrei Zagorsky's article in *Moscow News*, No.9, 1-8 March 1992, p.12.

RUSSIA AND TRANSCAUCASIA

The Georgian Conflicts

Since the break up of the Soviet Union, Georgia has provided the stage for three separate conflicts. Firstly, an armed struggle for power took place between the supporters and opponents of former president Zviad Gamsakhurdia, and the return of Eduard Shevardnadze as Georgia's leader in March 1992 was the culmination of the triumph of anti-Gamsakhurdia forces. The second conflict was the war between nationalist forces in South Ossetia and the central authorities in Tbilisi. A ceasefire was agreed upon between Russia, South Ossetia and Georgia in July 1992, and has been policed by forces from Russia, Georgia and both South Ossetia and the Russian republic of North Ossetia.

The third conflict is the war in Abkhazia between separatists and the Georgian government which was still continuing in early 1993. This war has been the most protracted, and has seriously strained relations between Russia and Georgia, as Tbilisi has accused Russia of supporting Abkhaz forces. The conflict has also coincided with negotiations for a bilateral Russo-Georgian treaty. Military issues have been very much to the fore in the treaty negotiations as Russian forces (ie. former Soviet forces) are still stationed in Georgia.

The Ossetian and Abkhaz conflagrations commenced long before the return of Shevardnadze. Gamsakhurdia also fought to retain Tbilisi's control of these regions, and Shevardnadze has shown a similar determination to use force to prevent the break up of Georgia.

The settlement reached in South Ossetia in July 1992 followed a meeting between Yeltsin and Shevardnadze in Dagomys in June. This agreement was preceded by aggressive rhetoric from Ruslan Khasbulatov and Rutskoy. Khasbulatov warned that Russia might annex South Ossetia and accused Georgia of 'genocide' against the Ossetian population. Khasbulatov said that the flow of refugees from South Ossetia to Russian meant that the conflict there could not be considered an internal problem of Georgia, and therefore since it directly affected Russian state interests, the Supreme Soviet 'may be forced to study' the question of South Ossetia's 'annexation to Russia'.[1] Rutskoy also accused the Georgian leadership of genocide and warned that Russia will not permit the conflict in South Ossetia to be resolved by force.[2]

Russian statements were partly motivated by concern that Russian forces may be caught up in the conflict. It also seemed, however, that Russian concerns went further, and represented an attempt to intimidate Georgia. Rutskoy's statement that Russia will not permit the conflict in Georgia to be resolved by force was an intrusion into Georgia's internal affairs, and carried the implication that Russia may use force.[3] Rutskoy's comments also revealed his lack of enthusiasm for the sovereignty of states from the 'near abroad'. He said that Russia did not wish to enter into a state of war with another ex-Soviet state, but he then asked: 'for how long must we tolerate everything that is going on in relation to the Russophone population in other republics...understand no one is entitled to say, today I am sovereign and tomorrow I will begin to knife, kill and shoot people'.[4] Georgia complained that one of Russia's deputy defence ministers, Georgy Kondratiev, visited Russian military bases in Georgia without obtaining the permission of the Georgian authorities. Russia denied that Kondratiev's visit had not been authorised. However, as already observed, unauthorised visits by Russian political and military leaders to various parts of the 'near abroad' have occurred more than once, and reveal scant respect for the sovereignty of these states.

Rutskoy feels that Russia should play a key role in resolving Georgia's internal conflicts, and that he sees the conflict as an opportunity to ensure that Georgia remains within a Russian sphere of influence. There is a strong Russian strategic interest in Georgia. Russia would appear to desire a pro-Russian state bordering Turkey, and as Russia can no longer feel confident that its navy will have access to Ukrainian naval facilities, Georgia's ports (though inferior to Ukraine's) become more important. Georgia also provides direct land access to Armenia, so providing a further reason for Russian strategic interest in Tbilisi.

A clearer admission of Russian strategic interest in Georgia has arisen from the Abkhaz conflict. Russia was again integrally involved in mediating and administering a ceasefire agreement in September 1992. The ceasefire failed to hold, however, and conflict intensified. By early 1993 Shevardnadze was accusing Russia of direct involvement in the conflict and saying that Georgia was at war with Russia. Russian defence minister Pavel Grachev (who visited Russian military facilities in February 1993, after which the Georgian government again claimed that this visit took place without the permission of the Georgian authorities) spoke of Russia's strategic interest in Georgia. Four days before his visit to Georgia he said that:

> As for the Russian troops, the armed force stationed in Batumi and Gudauta, this is a special matter. There is much that could be said about this. Just imagine the Black Sea coast of the Caucasus and the section where our troops are stationed...I will only say that this is a strategically important area for the Russian army. We have certain strategic interests there and must take every measure to ensure that our troops remain there; otherwise we will lose the Black Sea.[5]

Shevardnadze responded negatively to Grachev's comments on Russia's strategic interests, but Grachev claimed that his comments had been misinterpreted. However, when asked two weeks later about when Russian troops would be withdrawn from Abkhazia, Grachev commented:

> That is a decision for the political leadership. The defence minister does not decide this issue; however my point of view is, and I have said this, that there is a need for our forces to be there...I think that the Georgian people would not object to having Russian troops on their territory to defend Georgian sovereignty, among other things.[6]

Grachev's statements make clear Russia's strategic interest in Georgia. Russia is likely therefore to be reluctant to undertake a full withdrawal from Georgia, and will consequently demand to be involved in settling the internal ethnic disputes in Georgia, so as to legitimise a Russian presence there.

Armenia and Azerbaijan

The whole of Transcaucasia is likely to be of strategic importance to Russia. Armenia and Azerbaijan border on Iran and Turkey, significant Middle Eastern states that are, as Moscow is aware, becoming important actors in former Soviet Central Asia. Moscow's interest in developing relations with these states has grown since the break up of the Soviet Union, and Russia's desire for a cooperative relationship with Turkey and Iran means that it is likely that it will strive to maintain close relations with Armenia and Azerbaijan.

Russia accepts that Turkey will exert ever greater influence on Azerbaijan. Since the break up of the Soviet Union, Moscow has had no choice other than to accept the growing rapprochement between Baku and Ankara. Moscow has also been compelled to accept Azerbaijan's drift away from Moscow as a result of Abulfaz Elchibey's consolidation of power after assuming the presidency in June 1992. Under Elchibey, Azerbaijan has taken itself out of the CIS, saying that it never saw itself as a member. As Russia is concerned about the growth of Turkish influence throughout the Islamic regions of the former Soviet Union, then Moscow will be determined to retain some degree of influence in Azerbaijan.

Turkey and Iran have been extremely active in trying to mediate a settlement of the Nagorny Karabakh conflict, which makes it impossible for Russia to withdraw its interests in the region. If a settlement were to be reached without Russian involvement, this would amount to an abdication by Russia of its traditional presence in the region. Russia has therefore endeavoured to develop bilateral ties with Elchibey's Azerbaijan, despite his aversion to the CIS. The most significant breakthrough came with the signing of a Russo-Azerbaijan treaty in October 1992: the long term strategic direction of Azeri foreign policy is likely to be oriented towards Ankara, and Russian influence in Azerbaijan will be diminished.[7]

Russia's ties with Armenia will ensure continued access for Russia in the region: Russia has traditionally had a close relationship with Armenia, and Moscow will be determined to ensure Armenia's security, which faces serious challenges in the long term. As one observer writes, Armenia is 'bordered by an unreliable ally in the form of Georgia, an uneasy partner in the form of Iran, a hostile regional partner in the form of Turkey, and a declared enemy in the form of Azerbaijan.' Moscow's support is Erevan's only plausible source of protection. Armenia is accordingly an enthusiastic supporter of the Tashkent collective security agreement, and called for its implementation against Azerbaijan in June 1992.[8] Historical ties with Armenia and the desire to retain a presence in Transcaucasia mean that Russia will pursue the consolidation of an alliance with Erevan, and will endeavour to cooperate with Turkey in promoting a settlement of the Nagorny Karabakh conflict. However, if Turkish policy changes and Ankara provides greater support to Baku, Russia's relationship with Turkey is likely to deteriorate.[9]

Moldova

Moldova has been the scene of a civil war similar in nature to the wars in Georgia. The central government has been confronted with a separatist challenge in Transdnestr, and nationalist forces in Moscow have expressed support for the Transdnestrian leadership. As in the case of Georgia, the rhetoric between the Chisinau and Moscow has been extremely acrimonious.[10] Moldova declared independence from the Soviet Union in August 1991, after the failure of the anti-Gorbachev coup in Moscow. In the autumn of 1991, the leadership of the 'Dnestr Soviet Socialist Republic' launched an insurgency against the Moldovan government. Its President, Igor Smirnov, revealed in an interview at the beginning of 1992, that he wanted to see the restoration of both the Soviet Union and a single Soviet Army.[11] Fighting intensified in the first half of 1992 until peacekeeping forces were deployed in July 1992 following an agreement between Russia and Moldova, signed by Yeltsin and Moldovan president Mircea Snegur in Moscow. At the summit of Black Sea states in Istanbul in June 1992, Moldova agreed to grant more autonomy to Dnestr.[12]

The Dnestrian leadership fears that it would be swallowed up if Moldova and Romania were ever to be reunified. This is why it has resisted Chisinau's attempts to exert Moldovan sovereignty over the left bank. Moscow has not played the part of a neutral bystander, but through the presence of the 14th Army, it has intervened, so subverting the sovereignty of an independent state which is recognised by Russia. The 14th Army has supported, armed, and fought alongside the armed militias of the Dnestrian republic; as one observer expresses it, 'a symbiotic relationship has taken shape between the army and the Dnestr republic.'

The former commander of the 14th Army, Lieutenant General Gennady Yakovlev, was appointed by Smirnov as chief of defence of Dnestr in December 1991, until he was removed as 14th Army commander in January 1992. The former deputy chief of staff of the 14th Army, Colonel Stefan Kitsak, served as the commander of the Dnestr republican guard, and in July 1992, the commander of the Tiraspol garrison, Colonel Mikhail Bergman, was appointed as commander of the police and internal affairs troops of the Dnestrian republic. The leadership of the 14th Army and the Dnestr republic had jointly embarked on a merging of the 14th Army and the Dnestrian republican guard.

The 14th Army's support for the Dnestrian authorities became more overt after General Aleksandr Lebed was appointed as commander in June 1992. Lebed was outspoken in his support for the Dnestrian separatists, and fiercely condemned the policy of the Moldovan leadership. He described the Snegur leadership as fascist.[13] In an interview with *Literaturnaya Rossiya* in July 1992 he called for a Nuremberg trial of Moldova's leaders, and said that the Dnestr people have a right to this (ie. the 14th) army.[14] He then expressed his opinion on the future of Dnestr, which he saw as either joining the Russian Federation; its accession to a Russian Ukrainian state were such a state to be formed; or an independent state closely linked to Russia.[15] Lebed has also stated that Dnestr is an inalienable part of Russia, and that the CIS is an assemblage of abnormal states.[16]

Lebed's words constitute a flagrant violation of Moldovan sovereignty, and make nonsense of the Russian military leadership's claim that its armed forces stand outside politics. Grachev ordered Lebed to refrain from speaking to the media, although he was praised as a patriot by Gulko and by the current chief of the General Staff,

Mikhail Kolesnikov.[17] It is claimed that Yeltsin opposed the appointment of Lebed.[18] If so, Yeltsin's control over the Russian military is, to say the least, less than total.

Lebed opposed Romanian involvement in any settlement of the Moldovan crisis, arguing it should be resolved by the three former union republics, Moldova, Russia and Ukraine.[19]

Rutskoy became directly involved in the Moldovan conflict in April 1992, when he visited Dnestr and expressed support for the Dnestrian forces, calling for autonomy for Dnestr in a Moldovan federation. He also argued that the 14th Army should act as a peacekeeper, despite the fact that this army was involved in the fighting. Rutskoy's visit was criticised by Snegur who saw it as interference in Moldova's internal affairs. Rutskoy justified Russian interference in the Moldovan conflict by arguing that 'while following the course of non-interference in the affairs of other states, Russia must, at the same time, defend Russian and other citizens.[20] In June 1992 in the same rebuke he delivered to the Georgian leadership over Ossetia, he castigated the Moldovan government for committing genocide and warned that Russia would not allow Moldova to use force to resolve this conflict.[21]

Following the summit of Black Sea states in Istanbul in June 1992, Russia gained a diplomatic victory when the presidents of Moldova, Romania, Ukraine and Russia called upon the parliament of Moldova to examine and solve the problem of the status of the left bank of the Dnestr.[22] Burbulis warned in Istanbul that Russia was ready to apply economic sanctions against Moldova if it refused to grant federal status to Dnestr.[23] Snegur favours granting Moldova autonomy within a unitary state. Since the deployment of peacekeeping forces, Chisinau has offered the left bank Russians a substantial share of ministries in the Moldovan government, along with administrative autonomy and legal codification of Dnestr's right to secede if Moldova ever unites with Romania.[24]

The Moldovan government's willingness to grant autonomy and even the right of secession to Dnestr in the event of unification represents a triumph for Russian foreign policy in the region. The support rendered by the 14th Army to the Dnestr leadership and the criticism of the Moldovan leadership by Rutskoy, forced Yeltsin and Kozyrev to take greater interest in the fate of the Dnestr republic, and meant that Russia played an essential part in resolving what was a conflict taking place within the Moldovan state. The ceasefire agreement legitimises a Russian presence in Moldova, and the link between the Dnestr region and the Russian Federation enables Moscow to keep a toehold in Moldova. The 14th Army is likely to remain in Dnestr for several years, so reinforcing the link with Moscow.

There is a certain paradox to the support that Dnestr has received from Moscow. The Dnestrian leadership supported the abortive August 1991 coup as it supported the existence of the USSR. Two of Dnestr's staunchest defenders, Lebed and Rutskoy, both opposed the coup. However, both the Dnestr leadership and the nationalist camp in Moscow favour Russian predominance throughout the former Soviet Union. From the standpoint of the nationalist camp in Moscow, a Russian link with Dnestr may constrain any moves towards Moldovan Romanian unification. Yet, if unification does take place, Dnestr would be likely to separate, and, as Lebed suggested in *Literaturnaya Rossiya*, become linked in some way with Russia. This would enable Russia to maintain a territorial presence on Ukraine's south western flank and give Russia legitimate security interests in this region.

1 BBC, *SWB* SU/1408 B/5, 16 June 1992.

2 BBC, *SWB* SU/1413 C2/8, 20 June 1992. Rutskoy also directed his comments to the Moldovan government, at that time engaged in conflict with the pro-Moscow leaderhip in Dnestr.

3 Shevardnadze accused Russian forces of participating in the Ossetian conflict BBC, *SWB* SU/1414 C2/1, 23 June 1992. He also accused Rutskoy of threatening to bomb Georgian cities. See BBC, *SWB* SU/1415 C3/1, 24 June 1992.

4 BBC, *SWB*, SU/1414 C1/3, 23 June 1992.

5 BBC, *SWB* SU/1622 C1/6, 25 February 1993.

6 BBC, *SWB* SU/1625 B/7, 1 March 1993. Note that Russian forces are to be withdrawn by 1995 and border troops by 1994. See BBC *SWB* SU/1660 B/13, 12 April 1993.

7 In February 1993, the Azerbaijani defence ministry claimed that Russian troops aided Armenian forces in Nagorny Karabakh, *RFE/RL News Briefs* 15-19 February 1993 p.6.

8 *Los Angeles Times*, 17 June 1992.

9 See the Turkish prime minister's criticism of Russia in *The Independent*, 8 April 1993.

10 In June 1992, Moldovan President Mircea Snegur declared that Russia was at war with Moldova. See BBC, *SWB* SU/SU1414 C1/3, 23 June 1992.

11 *Krasnaya Zvezda*, 1 January 1992.

12 See the discussion below.

13 *Sovetskaya Rossiya*, 7 July 1992.

14 *Literaturnaya Rossiya*, No.31, 31 July 1992, p.2. Lebed has also criticised Yeltsin's foreign policy. In a news conference in Tiraspol on 4 July, he atttacked the policy of 'going with an outstretched hand to the world's cabinets, instead of building up a great power capable of imposing its will'. See *RFE/RL Research Report*, Vol.1, No.29, 17 July 1992, pp.73-74

15 *Literaturnaya Rossiya, op. cit.*

16 See *RFE/RL Research Report*, Weekly Review, Vol.1, No.29, 17 July 1992, p.73. Kozyrev also shares the view that Dnestr might one day become a part of Russia, *Le Monde*, 7-8 June 1992.

17 *Izvestiya*, 9 July 1992.

18 *Nezavisimaya Gazeta*, 4 August 1992.

19 BBC, *SWB* SU/1421 C1/1 1 July 1992. Lebed's opposition to Romanian involvement displays the aversion felt by many Russians to involvement by 'distant foreign' states in conflict resolution within the former Soviet Union.

20 BBC, *SWB* SU/1350 C1/4, 8 April 1992.

21 Ambartsumov said in a TV interview on 22 June 1992, that he agreed with Rutskoy's views on Moldova and Georgia, and contended that changes in the borders of newly independent states could be justified by the 'general geo-political interests of Russia', *RFE/RL Research Report*, Weekly Review, Vol.1, No.27, 3 July 1992, p.72.

22 BBC, *SWB* SU/1419 C2/1, 29 June 1992.

23 BBC, *SWB* SU/1418 C1/2, 27 June 1992.

24 Vladimir Socor 'Moldova's New 'Government of National Consensus', *RFE/RL Research Report*, Vol.1, No.47, 27 November 1992, pp.7-8.

CONCLUSION

It should be clear that a strong consensus exists in the Russian foreign and defence policy community that views the 'near abroad', or 'post Soviet geo-political space', as a Russian sphere of influence. Even the more liberal and pro-western members of this community are uncomfortable about the break up of the Soviet Union and the growth of political economic and military influence by states from the 'far abroad'. This is compounded by the sudden 'loss' of the Soviet position in Eastern Europe in 1989. Moscow's foreign policymakers have to accept the 'loss' of Eastern Europe. They currently lack sufficient foreign policy instruments to reverse this state of affairs, and are unlikely to be able do so for many years to come, if ever.

They are less likely to accept the loss of the fourteen republics of the ex-Soviet Union, and despite the manifold weaknesses of the Russian Federation, they are probably powerful enough to attempt to establish a *Pax Russica* throughout the 'near abroad'. The weakness of the Russian executive could mean that Moscow may pursue conflicting policies, with the military (or at least elements of it) acting independently of the political leadership in Moscow.

It is also possible that the continuing decline in Russian economic and military power may make it impossible for Moscow to exert effective control throughout the former Soviet Union. As discussed above, it is quite conceivable that the Russian Federation may break up, so making it impossible for the Russian state to pursue a coherent foreign policy.

In the meantime, however, Moscow's aspiration to retain the 'near abroad' as a Russian sphere of influence will constitute one of the key objectives of Russian foreign policy. Rutskoy's words 'that once the Russian flag has been raised it should never be lowered' is likely to shape Russian perceptions of, and policy towards, the former Soviet Union. This sphere of influence cannot be as tightly controlled as the old Soviet Union was able to control the Warsaw Pact states of Eastern Europe during the Cold War. Russian influence may be predominant in some regions, but it is unlikely ever to be exclusive.

'Distant foreign' states are likely to secure durable spheres of influence throughout many parts of the former Soviet Union.

A likely method of trying to ensure Russian predominance is by arguing that Russia should play the major role in peacekeeping operations throughout the former Soviet Union. The break up of the Soviet Union has engendered scores of potential ethnic and territorial disputes throughout the ex-USSR. If Russia plays the key role in settling these disputes and organising peacekeeping operations through CIS structures, then it may be able to ensure that its influence remains predominant, and construct a community of states in the former USSR around Russia. Moscow would thus become the security manager of the former Soviet Union. Yeltsin expressed this view in February 1993, in a speech he made to the Civic Union (which is likely to prove a responsive audience to such proposals). He said:

> Stopping all conflicts on the territory of the former USSR is Russia's vital interest. The world community sees more and more clearly Russia's special responsibility in this difficult undertaking. I believe the time has come for distinguished international organisations, including the UN, to grant Russia special powers of a guarantor of peace and stability in regions of the former USSR.[1]

This paragraph was preceded by a call for the development of confederal-type relations with other CIS states. Yeltsin's statement is similar to the call in the Civic Union's political programme for Russia to play a special role in preventing conflicts in the former Soviet Union.[2] The major difference is that the Civic Union wishes to go further than Yeltsin, as its programme talks of Russia's role in preventing conflicts in the former USSR and the adjoining regions, which could conceivably include former Eastern Europe and the Middle East regions that fall within Rogov's second circle of Russian foreign policy interests.[3]   Indeed the former communist states of Eastern Europe are likely to be viewed by Moscow as part of its sphere of influence. Vladislav Chernov, the deputy chief of the administration of strategic security in the security council has referred to the East European states as forming part of a Russian 'sphere of interests'.[4] Just as Yeltsin calls on the UN to grant Russia this special role, so the Civic Union calls for American recognition of Russia's role.

Russian policy is therefore calling for the West to accept the former Soviet Union as its sphere of influence. It has been seen that Ambartsumov has called for a Russian Monroe Doctrine throughout the former Soviet Union. The chairman of the Supreme Soviet Foreign Affairs Committee has linked this to the West granting Russia the role of peacemaker throughout this area. In August 1992 he argued that:

> As the internationally recognised legal successor to the USSR, the Russian Federation's foreign policy must be based on a doctrine that proclaims the entire geo-political space of the former Soviet Union a sphere of vital interests (following the example of the US 'Monroe Doctrine in Latin America). Furthermore, it is necessary to obtain from the world community understanding and recognition of Russia's special interests in this space. Likewise, Russia must secure from the international community the role of political and military guarantor of stability on all the territory of the former USSR. It is therefore necessary to obtain the support of the G 7 countries for those functions of Russia up to hard currency subsidies for rapid response forces (Russian 'blue helmets').[5]

Two Russian interests thus appear to be emerging. One is the use of peacekeeping to ensure Russian influence throughout the former Soviet Union. The other is the wish to secure western acceptance of Russia's right to regard the 'near abroad' as its sphere of influence, and this is linked to a desire to keep the West out of peacekeeping operations in the former USSR. Both conservatives and liberals share this opinion. In July 1992, Kozyrev said:

> 'This [ie. the former Soviet Union] is after all our zone of responsibility and it is we who should find the forces to play the disengagement role. There is no need for us to rely on NATO and the WEU in this instance.'[6]

The commander of the CIS forces, Shaposhnikov has also opposed the presence of peacekeeping troops from NATO or from outside the CIS.[7]

Economic sanctions and peacekeeping operations have been discussed as levers by which Russia could exert its influence throughout the former Soviet Union. Some politicians have also called for military force to be used to protect Russians throughout the former Soviet Union, and Ambartsumov has hinted strongly that he supports this idea. In an interview with *Narodny Deputat* in 1992, he talked about the need for Russia to protect all those who live in the former USSR who 'look at Russia with hope'. He then commented that 'I do not justify such actions, but when one American officer was killed the United State then invaded Panama'. He then referred to a decree of the Congress of Peoples' Deputies about prohibiting the use of Russian troops outside of Russia, and warned that 'in so doing problems and geo-political interests have been forgotten again.' He links this with the decline of Russian influence in the former Soviet Union.[8]

When speaking in the Russian Congress of Peoples' Deputies in April 1992 on his visit to Dnestr, Rutskoy urged that Russia guarantee to defend its citizens wherever they live, and urged that Russia learn 'from the example of the USA' in protecting their nationals.[9] The reference to the US is probably, like Ambartsumov's comments, an expression of support for the use of military force to protect Russians and those who 'look at Russia with hope'.[10]

A more drastic advocacy of military force came from an article in *Diplomatichesky Vestnik*, the journal of the Russian Foreign Ministry, by Sergey Karagonov who was appointed a member of the Presidential Council in February 1993. Karaganov argued that Russia must fulfil its traditional role within the territory of the former Russian Empire, pressurising local leaders and if necessary sending in troops.[11] This does not represent official Russian policy, but it does reflect a direction that Russian policy could take. Kozyrev's references to sending peacekeeping troops to the Baltic states has already been discussed, and Yeltsin warned Snegur in June 1992 that Russia might intervene in the Moldovan conflict.[12] The Russian military leadership has placed great emphasis on creating highly mobile rapid reaction forces in its plans for reforming the Russian army, and these forces, if successfully created, could be used to intervene to protect those who look to Moscow.[13]

The possibility that Russia could use economic and military force to protect Russian and Russophone communities, or indeed any ethnic grouping on the territory of the former Soviet Union, could pressurise states of the 'near abroad' to tailor their foreign policies to Moscow's taste. A state that veered too far away from Moscow in its foreign policy orientation might be deemed as threatening to those ethnic groupings in the near abroad that Moscow feels obliged to protect. A form of 'Finlandisation' could emerge in some states in that they would pursue a largely independent foreign policy that nonetheless deferred to Moscow on key security issues.[14] It would probably effectively allow Moscow the right of veto over their own security policies. A new Brezhnev doctrine of limited sovereignty would thus emerge on the territory of the former Soviet Union in the interests of maintaining stability in the former Soviet geo-political space.[15]

How would the West respond to the establishment of a Russian sphere of influence in the former Soviet Union? It is evident that Russian policymakers look to the international community, and particularly the West, to legitimise what Ambartsumov terms 'Russia's Monroe Doctrine'. It is likely that Russian leaders would argue that, as the West is interested in seeing stability in the region of the former Soviet Union, and as Russia is the largest state in that region, then it is logical to grant Russia the right and responsibility to ensure stability.

Western policy certainly opposed the break up of the Soviet Union. President Bush's now infamous speech in Kiev in August 1991, attacking 'suicidal nationalism', epitomised Western policy at that time. After the failure of the *putsch* against Gorbachev, when centrifugal trends accelerated in the union republics, an uncertain situation arose in the Soviet Union. This preference remained after the failed coup of August 1991, when it was uncertain whether the Soviet Union would survive, with western states preferring to retain the existence of the all-union centre. When the Soviet Union was finally terminated in December 1991, the West's preference for the old Soviet Union was transferred to the CIS.

The West's main concern was for the security of the Soviet strategic nuclear weapons that were deployed outside of Russia, namely in Ukraine, Belarus and Kazakhstan. It was feared that Ukraine and Kazakhstan could assume control of these weapons and emerge as new nuclear powers. This uncertainty over the nuclear arsenal was translated into a desire to retain a 'central' authority that could maintain control over the weapons. After the demise of the USSR, the CIS effectively became the framework for this retention of 'central' control of the nuclear weapons. As the launch codes were in the physical possession of the military and political leadership in Moscow, Russia became the most important nuclear power, and the CIS agreed that Russia would ultimately become the sole nuclear power. The West supported these moves, preferring to deal with one nuclear decision-making centre (ie. Russia) rather than four possible alternatives.

Might this preference for one nuclear centre spill over into other areas of policy? Another reason why the West favoured the existence of the USSR was the belief that it provided an umbrella for a large number of potential conflicts that could emerge (and in many cases have emerged) on the territory of the former Soviet Union.[16] The experience of the break up of Yugoslavia in 1991 has given the West new security problems to face in Europe, as well as revealing that the West has been at a loss to know how to contend with these problems. The fear of new 'Yugoslavias' in the former Soviet Union is likely to create a western preference for Russian geo-political predominance in the 'near abroad'.[17]

The West tacitly accepted the Soviet Union's dominance of Eastern Europe during the years of the Cold War largely because it lacked the power to challenge the USSR in this region. The 'rollback' policy of the Eisenhower Administration was no more than rhetoric. Its failure to support the anti-communist resistance in Hungary in 1956 underlined how far the West had conceded Eastern Europe to the Soviet Union. By the mid 1970s, this policy had been modified by the so-called Sonnenfeldt doctrine, under which the US advocated, in the words of Helmut Sonnenfeldt, encouraging 'organic unity' between Eastern Europe and Moscow by adopting a policy capable of 'responding to the clearly visible aspirations in Eastern Europe for a more autonomous existence within the context of a strong Soviet geo-political influence.'[18]

Geo-political reality forced the West to accept the Brezhnev doctrine, and geo-political reality is likely to force the West to be persuaded by Russian arguments that it play the role of *gendarme* in the 'near abroad'. Fear of antagonising Russia as it defines its post-communist identity is likely to persuade the West to grant Russia this role, in which case the West would inevitably be relegating the ex-Soviet states to the status of Russian clients. In short, the only former Soviet state whose sovereignty and independence the West would really accept would be that of the Russian Federation. The West might therefore subconsciously adopt a new version of the Sonnenfeldt doctrine, encouraging 'organic unity' between Moscow and the 'near abroad' that would endeavour to respond 'to the clearly visible aspirations in the 'near abroad' for a more autonomous existence within the context of a strong Russian geo-political influence.

It has been seen that Russia's policy towards the 'near abroad' has been the subject of contention between the advocates of loose and tight hegemony, with Kozyrev arguing that diplomacy constitutes the best means of protecting Russians and Russophones, and Rutskoy, who is the more enthusiastic advocate of economic and politico-military pressure. It is becoming increasingly difficult for Kozyrev to hold the line against his conservative opponents, and if a nationalist leadership were to emerge in Russia, then the West may face a Russia which poses a more direct threat to the security of its neighbours.

The West would then face the question of how seriously it takes the security of states such as Ukraine and the Baltic states. If the views of Karaganov ever became official policy, what would the reaction of the West be? Would it extend security guarantees to these state, so embarking on overtly anti-Russian policy? Would it invite these states (but not Russia) to join NATO? This would mark a return to containment, but this time extending the boundaries of containment to the borders of the Russian Federation. It would also be an anti-

Russian policy measure that the West would be reluctant to undertake. Yet if this situation ever does arise, then the West is likely to be in the position of having to choose either between conceding this area to Russia or making an overt security commitment to the ex-Soviet states. Adequate security structures exist in neither East Central Europe nor the former Soviet Union. The expansion of CSCE membership to incorporate all the former Soviet states, and the establishment of the North Atlantic Cooperation Council, do not provide the necessary security structures, and the West may find that in the area of the former Soviet Union it will be tacitly endorsing a *Pax Russica* as the basic security institution for that region, despite the fact that this will be to the detriment of the security interests of many of the states of the 'near abroad'.

1 BBC, *SWB* SU/1626 B/1, 2 March 1993.
2 *Ibid*. Karaganov also argues that the CSCE should allot Russia this role within the CIS in *Diplomatichesky Vestnik*, No 21-22, 15-30 November 1992, p.43-45.
3 See Rogov's article in *SSHA: Ekonomika, Politika, Ideologiya*, October 1992, p.8.
4 See Chernov's article 'Russia's national interests and the threats to her security', Nezavisimaya Gazeta, 29 April 1993.
5 *Izvestiya*, 7 August 1992.
6 BBC, *SWB* SU/1431 C1/3, 13 July 1992.
7 *Krasnaya Zvezda*, 23 June 1992.
8 See the interview with Ambartsumov in *Narodny Deputat*, No.16, 1992, especially p.17.
9 BBC, *SWB* SU/1350 C1/4-5, 8 April 1992.
10 Rutskoy is rumoured to have seriously considered sending troops to Moldova to halt fighting in June 1992. See *Nezavisimaya Gazeta*, 1 July 1992.
11 See Karaganov's article in *Diplomatichesky Vestnik, op cit*.
12 *International Herald Tribune*, 22 June 1992. See also the article by Sergey Stankevich in *Rossiskaya Gazeta*, 23 June 1992.
13 See Grachev's outline of his reform plans for the Russian armed forces in *Krasnaya Zvezda*, 21 July 1992. For more on rapid reaction forces see also *Krasnaya Zvezda*, 18 December 1992, *Rossiskie Vesti*, 6 March 1993. In *Krasnaya Zvezda*, 23 February 1993, Yeltsin warned that Russia faced a